Differentiated Containment

U.S. Policy Toward Iran and Iraq

Differentiated Containment

U.S. Policy
Toward Iran and Iraq

*Report of an Independent Task Force
Sponsored by the
Council on Foreign Relations*

Zbigniew Brzezinski and Brent Scowcroft,
Co-Chairs
Richard W. Murphy, Project Director

Also Includes

Statement and Recommendations of an Independent
Study Group on Gulf Stability and Security

The Council on Foreign Relations, Inc., a nonprofit, nonpartisan national membership organization founded in 1921, is dedicated to promoting understanding of international affairs through the free and civil exchange of ideas. The Council's members are dedicated to the belief that America's peace and prosperity are firmly linked to that of the world. From this flows the mission of the Council: to foster America's understanding of its fellow members of the international community, near and far, their peoples, cultures, histories, hopes, quarrels, and ambitions; and thus to serve, protect, and advance America's own global interests through study and debate, private and public.

THE COUNCIL TAKES NO INSTITUTIONAL POSITION ON POLICY ISSUES AND HAS NO AFFILIATION WITH THE U.S. GOVERNMENT. ALL STATEMENTS OF FACT AND EXPRESSIONS OF OPINION CONTAINED IN ALL ITS PUBLICATIONS ARE THE SOLE RESPONSIBILITY OF THE AUTHOR OR AUTHORS.

The Council on Foreign Relations will sponsor independent Task Forces from time to time when it believes that a current foreign policy or international economic debate of critical importance to the United States can benefit from the advice of a small group of people of divergent backgrounds and views. Most, but not all, Task Force members are also members of the Council, and the Council provides the group with staff support.

The goal of the Task Force is to reach a consensus on the issue; if a strong and meaningful consensus cannot be reached, the goal is to state concisely alternative positions.

A Study Group consists of a series of sessions over an extended period of time for the in-depth examination of a complicated U.S. policy problem requiring step-by-step analysis of its principal component parts.

The Statements of both the Task Force and Study Group reflect the general policy thrust and judgments reached by each group, although not all members necessarily subscribe fully to every finding and recommendation.

For further information about the Council or this Task Force, please contact the Public Affairs Office, Council on Foreign Relations, 58 East 68th Street, New York, NY 10021.

CONTENTS

[v]

FOREWORD AND ACKNOWLEDGMENTS

Since World War II, the United States has identified the security and stability of the Gulf region as a vital national interest. This publication presents two documents. The first, *Differentiated Containment: U.S. Policy Toward Iran and Iraq*, is the report of the Co-Chairs of an Independent Task Force sponsored by the Council on Foreign Relations. The report, by Zbigniew Brzezinski and Brent Scowcroft, serves as the Statement of the Task Force and also appeared in the May/June 1997 issue of *Foreign Affairs*. The second document, *Gulf Stability and Security and Its Implications for U.S. Foreign Policy*, contains the Statement and Recommendations of an Independent Study Group also sponsored by the Council. As defined in these two documents, the Gulf region includes Iran, Iraq, and the members states of the Gulf Cooperation Council—Bahrain, Kuwait, Oman, Qatar, Saudi Arabia, and the United Arab Emirates.

The Task Force met four times in 1996–97. Its Co-Chairs traveled to the region in March 1997 to make their first-hand review of the situation. The Study Group met seven times in 1996, and its deliberations were summarized in a report drafted by Dr. Shibley Telhami of Cornell University. Neither group achieved a full consensus on how the United States might better assist in maintaining Gulf security and stability, and some significant dissenting opinions have been noted. The groups' reports provide a number of recommendations for Washington's consideration that we hope will receive serious attention.

For those interested in examining the context of current U.S. policy toward the Gulf, the Background Materials section of this publication provides a variety of primary sources. They include official documents and statements of the U.N. Security Council and the U.S. government; a *Foreign Affairs* article by Anthony Lake, assistant to the president for national security affairs from 1993 to 1997; an article on Iran by an Israeli defense analyst; a press interview with the German foreign minister concerning the German court verdict in the so-called Mykonos case; excerpts from the March 1997 communiqué of the foreign ministers of the Gulf Cooperation Council; and a summary of a recent conference on Gulf security held in Abu Dhabi.

As Project Director of the Independent Task Force and Chair of the earlier Independent Study Group, I wish to thank all participants for the time and thought they devoted to those proceedings. I particularly thank Nomi Colton-Max, the Program Associate for the Middle East at the Council, for the work she performed as rapporteur and editor of the Study Group report.

Richard W. Murphy
Hasib J. Sabbagh Senior Fellow for the Middle East

Differentiated Containment:
U.S. Policy Toward Iran and Iraq

STATEMENT OF THE INDEPENDENT TASK FORCE

The Persian Gulf is one of the few regions whose importance to the United States is obvious. The flow of Gulf oil will continue to be crucial to the economic well-being of the industrialized world for the foreseeable future; developments in the Gulf will have a critical impact on issues ranging from Arab-Israeli relations and religious extremism to terrorism and nuclear nonproliferation. Every president since Richard Nixon has recognized that ensuring Persian Gulf security and stability is a vital U.S. interest.

The Clinton administration's strategy for achieving this goal during the president's first term was its attempted "dual containment" of Iraq and Iran. This is more a slogan than a strategy, however, and the policy may not be sustainable for much longer. In trying to isolate both of the Gulf's regional powers, the policy lacks strategic viability and carries a high financial and diplomatic cost. Saddam Hussein is still in power six years after his defeat at the hands of a multinational coalition, and the international consensus on continuing the containment of Iraq is fraying. The strident U.S. campaign to isolate Iran, in turn, drives Iran and Russia together and the United States and its Group of Seven allies apart. Finally, the imposing U.S. military presence that helps protect the members of the Gulf Cooperation Council (GCC) from external threats is being exploited by hostile elements to take advantage of internal social, political, and economic problems. The advent of the Clinton administration's second term, together with the imminent inauguration of a new administration in Iran following this May's elections, provides an oppor-

This Statement was published under the byline of the two Co-Chairs, Zbigniew Brzezinski and Brent Scowcroft, and the Project Director, Richard Murphy, in the May/June 1997 issue of *Foreign Affairs*. The Task Force members are signatories to this Statement. This Statement reflects the general policy thrust and judgments reached by the Task Force, although not all members of the group necessarily subscribe to every finding and recommendation. Additional views of members of the Task Force appear in the footnotes.

[3]

tunity to review U.S. policies toward the Gulf and consider whether midcourse corrections could improve the situation.

The first step in such a reevaluation is to view the problems in the Gulf clearly and objectively. In Iraq, the United States confronts a police state led by an erratic tyrant whose limited but potentially serious capacity for regional action is currently subject to constraint. In Iran, the United States confronts a country with potentially considerable military and economic capabilities and an imperial tradition, which occupies a crucial position both for the Gulf and for future relations between the West and Central Asia. If Iraq poses a clear and relatively simple immediate threat, Iran represents a geopolitical challenge of far greater magnitude and complexity.

Consultation with leaders of some Persian Gulf countries has made it plain to us that they do not share an identical view of the threat posed by Iraq and Iran. Hence no U.S. Gulf policy will satisfy everyone in every respect. That makes it all the more essential that any adjustment in U.S. policy toward Iraq and Iran be preceded by extensive consultations with friendly Gulf leaders. Inadequate dialogue and unilateral action have caused some insecurity in the region and weakened trust in U.S. steadfastness.

PERSISTENT PROBLEMS

When the British withdrew from the Persian Gulf in 1971, the United States became the principal foreign power in the region. For almost three decades it has pursued the goal of preserving regional stability, using a variety of means to that end, particularly regarding the northern Gulf powers of Iraq and Iran.

At first the United States relied on Iran as its chief regional proxy, supporting the shah's regime in the hope that it would be a source of stability. This policy collapsed in 1979 with the Iranian Revolution, when Iran switched from staunch ally to implacable foe. During the 1980s, the United States strove to maintain a de facto balance of power between Iraq and Iran so that neither would be able to achieve a regional hegemony that might threaten American interests. The United States provided some help to Iraq during the Iran-Iraq War of 1980–88, moved in other ways to counter the spread of Iranian-backed Islamic militancy, and provided—with Israeli encouragement—some help to Iran, chiefly in the context of seeking the release of American hostages. This era ended with Iraq invading Kuwait in 1990 and the United States leading an international coalition to war to restore Kuwaiti sovereignty and defeat Iraq's bid for dominance. ·

The Clinton administration came into office in 1993 facing the challenge of ensuring Gulf stability in a new international and regional environment. The disappearance of the Soviet Union gave the United States unprecedented freedom of action, while the Madrid Conference, sponsored by the Bush administration, inaugurated a fundamentally new phase of the Middle East peace process, offering hope that the Arab-Israeli conflict might eventually prove solvable. The Clinton team's initial Middle East policy had two aspects: continued support for the peace process and dual containment of Iraq and Iran. These strands were seen as reinforcing each other: keeping both Iraq and Iran on the sidelines of regional politics, the administration argued, would protect Saudi Arabia and the smaller Gulf monarchies and enable Israel and the moderate Arab states to move toward peace, while the burgeoning Arab-Israeli détente would demonstrate that the attitudes of the "rejectionist front" were costly and obsolete.

Dual containment was envisaged not as a long-term solution to the problems of Gulf stability but as a way of temporarily isolating the two chief opponents of the American-sponsored regional order. Regarding Iraq, the policy involved maintaining the full-scale international economic sanctions and military containment the administration had inherited, including a no-fly zone in southern Iraq and a protected Kurdish enclave in the north. The Clinton administration stated that it merely sought Iraqi compliance with the post–Gulf War U.N. Security Council resolutions, particularly those mandating the termination of Iraq's weapons of mass destruction programs. In practice, the administration made it clear that it had no intention of dealing with Saddam Hussein's regime, and seemed content, for lack of a better alternative, to let Iraq stew indefinitely. The administration responded to Iraqi provocations, but saw little opportunity to oust Saddam except at great cost in blood and treasure.

The dual containment policy initially involved mobilizing international political opposition against Iran, together with limited unilateral economic sanctions. The Clinton administration asserted that it was not trying to change the Iranian regime per se but rather its behavior, particularly its quest for nuclear weapons, its support for terrorism and subversion in the region, and its opposition to the peace process. By early 1995, however, the U.S. attitude toward Iran began to harden. The Iranian behavior at issue had continued. But the real impetus for a shift seems to have come out of American domestic politics, in particular the administration's desire to head off a challenge on Iran policy mounted by an increasingly bellicose Republican Congress.

Congressional initiatives were designed to increase pressure on so-called rogue states such as Iran and Libya, to the point of erecting secondary boycotts against all parties doing business with them, including American allies. Hoping to deflate support for such action, in spring 1995 President Clinton announced (with an eye on domestic politics at the World Jewish Congress) that he was instituting a complete economic embargo against Iran. The move achieved its intended domestic effects in the United States, but only temporarily. Late in 1995 pressure from Congressional Republicans, led by House Speaker Newt Gingrich (R-Ga.), called for covert action against the Iranian regime, and last year Congress passed the Iran and Libya Sanctions Act, which the president signed. This legislation mandates U.S. sanctions against any foreign firm that invests more than $40 million in a given year in the development of energy resources in Iran or Libya. Not surprisingly, it has been strenuously opposed by America's allies as an unjustifiable attempt to coerce them into following a hard-line policy.

At the start of President Clinton's second term, therefore, U.S. Persian Gulf policy is at an impasse. Saddam Hussein remains in power in Iraq and has even regained some control over the Kurdish areas of the north, while the Gulf War coalition that defeated him is eroding. Toughened U.S. sanctions against Iran, although doing some damage to the Iranian economy, have produced no major achievements and increasingly isolate America rather than their target. The continued willingness and ability of some members of the GCC and others to help implement these policies is open to question. What, then, is to be done?

The continued rule of Saddam Hussein poses a danger to the stability and security of the region. He has threatened his neighbors while doing everything possible to acquire weapons of mass destruction in direct violation of international law, even during the last several years, when subject to the most restrictive supervision in the history of international arms control. Although there are real costs involved in maintaining Iraq's pariah status, it is difficult to see how any policy in the military sphere other than continued containment can be adopted so long as Saddam remains in power. The United States should be prepared to maintain Iraq's military containment unilaterally should the will of others falter. Similarly, while there are costs to keeping Iraq's oil off the world market, retaining the economic embargo in general is necessary, because with unrestricted access to large profits Saddam would likely embark on further military development.

The United States may, however, need to consider a revised approach to the political and economic aspects of Iraq's containment, because not all of them can be implemented unilaterally. Furthermore, they have unfortunate consequences on the humanitarian situation in Iraq, which especially concerns some members of the GCC. While America's basic goal should continue to be keeping Saddam's Iraq in a straitjacket, the United States may need to adjust the fit to ensure the straitjacket holds. There should thus be five corollaries to the basic containment policy, not all of which the Clinton administration has adequately stressed.

First, the international community must credibly demonstrate its concern for the Iraqi people even if their own ruler does not. Sanctions against Iraq continue to be necessary, but the United States and others should try to mitigate the sanctions' effects on ordinary Iraqis. The offer to permit Iraq to sell some oil and use the proceeds to alleviate its humanitarian problems has been on the table since the end of the Gulf War and remains a good idea. Saddam's recent willingness to accept stringent conditions on the disbursement of the funds from such oil sales has led to the deal enshrined in U.N. Security Council Resolution 986, which was designed to address this problem. If it becomes necessary or appropriate to ease Iraq's economic containment, the sanctions should be suspended rather than lifted completely, so that the international community can easily reimpose them should unacceptable Iraqi behavior resume.[1]

Second, the United States should reassure Iraqis and their neighbors that while America continues to seek political relief for the Iraqi people, it is committed to the integrity of the Iraqi state. The ultimate goal of U.S. policy should be an Iraq that retains its existing borders and that at some point after Saddam has left the scene can take its rightful place as a legitimate member of the international community. Any doubts about this should be dispelled.

Third, the United States should consult more closely with Turkey on areas of common interest. Turkey's continued support for U.S. policy in northern Iraq is crucial, and to secure it Washington should confer on how best to stabilize the situation in Iraqi Kurdistan. If the Turks are not comfortable with the status quo, including the arrangements for Operation Northern Watch, the United States should discuss with them what might be done to address their concerns.

Fourth, the United States should send a clear signal that it is prepared to work with a post-Saddam Iraqi regime. That such a regime be benign and democratic is desirable but unlikely, so these factors should not be prerequisites for Iraq's reintegration into regional politics. American officials should state that they would be prepared to deal with any Iraqi regime—including one that emerged from within the military or the Baath Party—that is ready to fulfill Iraq's basic international obligations. To start relations from as clean a slate as possible, the United States should consult with interested parties about whether a post-Saddam regime should be

---

[1] Phebe A. Marr and Robin Wright do not think that sanctions have to be suspended to be eased. They maintain that U.N. Resolution 986 provides an appropriate vehicle for increasing future oil revenues for Iraq while maintaining controls on Saddam.

offered relief from Iraq's enormous debts or Gulf War reparations. Such a gesture would be a sensible way to deal with the problems of Iraqi reconstruction, and it might even help induce aspiring successors to step forward.

Fifth, if and when Saddam's regime crosses clearly drawn lines of appropriate behavior, particularly with regard to its weapons of mass destruction programs and its threats to other countries, the United States should punish it severely and effectively. For several years the United States has responded to Iraqi provocations with more bluster than action; the precedent of Operation Desert Storm shows the reverse is a better strategy. With his behavior incurring militarily insignificant penalties, Saddam may have concluded that he can continue to maneuver with relative impunity to heighten the contradictions in the allied coalition. This cat-and-mouse game should stop. There must be no doubt in anyone's mind that should Saddam try to break his containment through force, he will be punished. Accompanying such resolve must be a serious diplomatic effort to nurse the Gulf War coalition of European and Arab countries and Japan back to robust health. Forceful American action can and should build on multilateral consultation and a sense of purpose and necessity; it should not be conditioned on allied approval, but neither should the United States be perceived as ignoring allies' concerns or taking their support for granted.

BEYOND HOSTILE FANATICISM

Iran's geopolitical importance is greater than Iraq's, and the challenge it represents is more complex. Given the American military presence, Iran does not currently pose a threat of military aggression, but its long-term policies could destabilize the region.

Several areas of Iran's behavior are frequently cited as sources of concern: its conventional military buildup, its opposition to the peace process, its promotion of Islamic militancy, its support of terrorism and subversion, and its quest for nuclear weapons. Terrorism and nuclear weapons, especially the latter, directly threaten U.S. national interests. Both issues, however, can be addressed by specific policy instruments, rather than the current crude and counterproductive attempt to cordon off the entire country. A more nuanced approach could yield greater benefits at lower cost.

Concerned about traditional military threats to regional security, some observers have worried about increases in Iran's conventional military capabilities. So far, there is little reason to believe that Iran's conventional military buildup will pose a direct challenge to U.S. regional supremacy. And for years to come, the United States will retain the capability to rebuff any such challenge.

Continued progress in the Middle East peace process is indeed an important American interest. Still, opposition to that process by another country should not be grounds for international excommunication. Israel itself has found it useful to have dealings with Iran on various occasions, most recently with the help of German mediation, and the United States should not feel constrained from doing the same when its interests so dictate.

Although Iran has often used religion as a cloak for subversion and terrorism, the United States must be careful not to demonize Islam, worrying simplistically about a "green menace" comparable to the old red one. The Iranian regime, unable to govern effectively, has lost appeal both at home and abroad. Sectarian, ethnic, and geographic cleavages within the Islamic world militate against the rise of a unified, Iranian-led threat.

Iran's support of violence and subversion abroad should, however, concern the United States. Iran has provided backing for terrorists and fomented unrest in other countries, and the international community should continue to harshly criticize Iran for these acts.[2] Direct attacks on American citizens would constitute a special provocation and call for clear retaliatory measures. As a response to terrorism in general, however, containment is not a solution.

The single most worrisome aspect of Iran's behavior is its apparent quest for a nuclear weapons capability. The United States

---

[2] On April 10, 1997, a German court ruled that a committee that included Iran's highest government leaders gave orders to carry out the slaying of three Kurdish dissidents at the Mykonos restaurant in Berlin in 1992. Wright comments that the outcome of the Mykonos trial presents both the justification and opening for joint action with our European allies in a number of ways.

should respond by pushing the controls and inspection provisions of the existing nuclear nonproliferation regime to their limits and continuing to make counter-proliferation efforts a top priority. It should focus more narrowly on the nuclear threat as opposed to other issues, which might strengthen its case for controls and achieve greater success in stemming the flow of support for the Iranian nuclear weapons program. Finally, it should explore the notion of using carrots in addition to sticks in getting Iran to shift course.

There seems little justification for the treatment the United States currently accords Iran because of its nuclear program. Instead of simply punishing the country, the United States should consider whether a tradeoff might be feasible in return for Iran's acceptance of restrictions on its civilian nuclear program or intrusive inspections by the International Atomic Energy Agency of its nuclear facilities. Since the economic rationale for nuclear power has diminished in recent years, it may be possible to get Iran to limit its civilian nuclear energy program enough to give outsiders reasonable confidence that further military progress is not being made. Such an outcome, possibly arranged with Chinese or Russian support, would leave both the United States and Iran better off and significantly ease tensions in the region.

The policy of unilateral U.S. sanctions against Iran has been ineffectual, and the attempt to coerce others into following America's lead has been a mistake. Extraterritorial bullying has generated needless friction between the United States and its chief allies and threatened the international free trade order that America has promoted for so many decades. To repair the damage and avoid further self-inflicted wounds, the United States should sit down with the Europeans, the Japanese, and its Gulf allies and hash out what each other's interests are, what policies make sense in trying to protect those interests, and how policy disagreements should be handled. Only such high-level consultation can yield multilateral policies toward Iran that stand a good chance of achieving their goals and being sustainable over the long term.

One negative consequence of current policy is the damage inflicted on America's interest in gaining greater access to the energy sources of Central Asia. An independent and economically accessible Central Asia is in the interests of both the United States and Iran. The United States should do nothing to preclude Central Asia's eventual emergence, nor stand in the way of deals that might facilitate it. The United States should therefore refrain from automatically opposing the construction of gas and oil pipelines across Iran. Here, as with policy toward Iraq, the United States must consult more often with its Turkish ally and fashion a regional policy that makes sense on the ground.

Another area of common interest is the resuscitation of U.S.-Iranian commercial relations. To this end, Washington should be open-minded regarding the resumption of activity by American oil companies in Iran. In 1995, for example, the U.S. government forced the cancellation of a $1 billion deal between Iran and Conoco; this served no one's interests except those of the French firm Total. Future commercial deals should be evaluated on an individual basis and permitted unless they contribute specifically to Iranian behavior the United States opposes.

A NUANCED CONTAINMENT

However one judges its achievements to date, dual containment cannot provide a sustainable basis for U.S. policy in the Persian Gulf. A more nuanced and differentiated approach to the region is in order, one in tune with America's longer-term interests. This new policy would keep Saddam boxed in, but would supplement such resolve with policy modifications to keep the Gulf War coalition united. The new policy would start with the recognition that the United States' current attempt at unilateral isolation of Iran is costly and ineffective and that its implementation, in the words of one recent study, "lacks the support of U.S. allies and is a leaky sieve." The United States should instead consider the possibilities of creative trade-offs, such as the relaxation of opposition to the Iranian nuclear program in exchange for rigid and comprehensive inspection and control procedures.

This new course would not involve a dramatic policy reversal and is not likely to yield vast benefits in the immediate future. What it would do is enable the United States to sustain its policy and keep options open for the long term. America may have to consider modifying certain aspects of Iraq's economic containment to keep its military straitjacket securely fastened. On the other hand, flexibility would facilitate diplomatic contacts, presuming an Iranian interest in better relations. Absent such statesmanship, it is all too likely that U.S. policy in the Gulf will continue to be driven by domestic political imperatives rather than national interests, with the hard line of recent years making long-term goals increasingly difficult to achieve.

The foundation of America's policy in the Persian Gulf should continue to be a commitment to ensuring the security of its allies and protecting the flow of oil. Few doubt that the United States has the power to sustain this commitment, but some question whether it has the will. In such circumstances, a recommitment by President Clinton to the principles of the Carter Doctrine—a renewal of U.S. vows to the Gulf—might be both welcome and appropriate. It is imperative that all parties understand an important strategic reality: the United States is in the Persian Gulf to stay. The security and independence of the region is a vital U.S. interest. Any accommodation with a post-Saddam regime in Iraq or with a less hostile government in Iran must be based on that fact.

MEMBERS OF THE INDEPENDENT TASK FORCE

ZBIGNIEW BRZEZINSKI, Co-Chair of the Task Force, is Counselor at the Center for Strategic and International Studies and Professor of American Foreign Policy at the Johns Hopkins School of Advanced International Studies. Dr. Brzezinski was the National Security Advisor to President Carter.

BRENT SCOWCROFT, Co-Chair of the Task Force, is President of the Scowcroft Group and the Founder and President of the Forum for International Policy. He was the National Security Advisor to Presidents Ford and Bush.

JOSEPH P. HOAR is President of J.P. Hoar and Associates and was the Commander in Chief of the U.S. Central Command. He is also the Chairman of the Middle East Forum of the Council on Foreign Relations.

PHEBE A. MARR† is a Senior Fellow at the Institute for National Strategic Studies, National Defense University. She is a scholar of the modern history of Iraq and Gulf politics.

RICHARD W. MURPHY is the Hasib J. Sabbagh Senior Fellow for the Middle East at the Council on Foreign Relations. He was the Assistant Secretary of State for Near Eastern and South Asian Affairs from 1983 to 1989.

WILLIAM B. QUANDT is the Byrd Professor of Government and Foreign Affairs at the University of Virginia. He served on the National Security Council staff in the Nixon and Carter administrations with responsibility for the Middle East.

JAMES SCHLESINGER is Counselor, Center for Strategic and International Studies. He has served as Secretary of Defense, Secretary of Energy, and Director of Central Intelligence.

---

†Individual largely concurs with the Statement but has endorsed one or more footnotes.
Note: Institutional affiliations are for identification purposes only.

SHIBLEY TELHAMI is Associate Professor of Government and Director of the Program for Contemporary Near Eastern Studies at Cornell University. He is also a Non-Resident Fellow at the Brookings Institution.

ROBIN WRIGHT† is the author of two books on Iran and is a former Mideast correspondent for *The Sunday Times* of London. She now covers global trends for *The Los Angeles Times*.

Staff

NOMI COLTON-MAX is Program Associate for the Middle East at the Council on Foreign Relations. She received an M.A. in international relations and economics from the Johns Hopkins School of Advanced International Studies.

DENNIS HEJLIK is a Military Fellow at the Council on Foreign Relations. He was a Battalion Commander with the Second Marine Division and is a veteran of Desert Storm.

GIDEON ROSE is a Fellow for National Security Policy at the Council on Foreign Relations. He served as Associate Director for Near East and South Asian Affairs on the National Security Council staff from 1994 to 1995.

---

†Individual largely concurs with the Statement but has endorsed one or more footnotes.
Note: Institutional affiliations are for identification purposes only.

Gulf Stability and Security and Its Implications for U.S. Foreign Policy

STATEMENT AND RECOMMENDATIONS OF THE INDEPENDENT STUDY GROUP

U.S. policy toward the states of the Persian Gulf is at an impasse. Maintenance of the policy known as dual containment concerning Iraq and Iran is producing uneven results, not all of them positive from the point of view of either U.S. interests or those of our friends among the Gulf states.

While Iraq is weakened militarily and poses no immediate threat to the region, Saddam Hussein remains in power in Baghdad. Some argue he is stronger today for having eliminated many real and suspected domestic challengers during the six years since Operation Desert Storm. Some even charge that the United States and certain of its close Arab partners are responsible for inflicting unnecessary suffering on the Iraqi people. But there is no sound basis for predicting how long Saddam Hussein will continue to maintain control.

Iran stridently opposes the Arab-Israeli peace process, which remains a major U.S. policy interest. In Washington's view, Tehran continues to sponsor international terrorism and to pursue a nuclear weapons program.[1] Iran's internal political situation has created no openings for a meaningful political dialogue with the American administration, and Washington has shown no interest in establishing such a dialogue.

American efforts to develop the defensive capabilities of Bahrain, Kuwait, Oman, Qatar, Saudi Arabia, and the United Arab Emirates

---

Members of the Study Group endorse the Statement and Recommendations except where their differing views are indicated in footnotes. Background information is provided in the Background Report that follows.

[1] The Study Group Statement, Recommendations, and Background Report were completed before the judgment of the German court in the Mykonos assassination trial. On April 10, 1997, the court ruled that Iran's highest government leaders gave orders to carry out the killing of three Kurdish dissidents at the Mykonos restaurant in Berlin in 1992. The ruling provided—and the impending conclusion of an investigation of the June 25, 1996, Al-Khobar bombing in Saudi Arabia may provide—powerful evidence of the direct involvement of the most senior Iranian leadership in international terrorism.

(the member-states of the Gulf Cooperation Council, GCC) continue. These states have bought substantial quantities of sophisticated equipment, primarily from the United States and European allies. But the GCC states have yet to build an effective defense system that would replace or significantly shrink the need for America to defend them against external aggression.[2]

Thus far the American public has accepted the administration's policy of dual containment of Iraq and Iran. This reflects widespread resentment of Iran's behavior since its 1979 revolution and deep distrust of Saddam Hussein since his invasion of Kuwait and his post-war attempts to evade U.N. controls on his weapons of mass destruction (WMD). There has been virtually no domestic challenge to maintenance of the present force levels and financial costs of the American investment in the policy of dual containment, and the administration has successfully argued that its military engagement in the Gulf serves to defend vital U.S. interests.

This could change. While the U.S. commitment to provide external security for the states of the GCC against Iraqi and Iranian aggression is firm, it may be too expensive to keep up indefinitely. Equally important, the U.S. military presence in the Gulf, which is intended to maintain security and stability, risks making the regimes the United States seeks to support a target for their domestic critics. Beyond a doubt the United States can defend the area against external aggression, but it cannot deal with domestic challenges to regimes' legitimacy.[3] The United States must explore alternatives that will better sustain American interests. Friends in the region face

---

[2] Anthony H. Cordesman asserts that the use of GCC as short-hand for individual southern Gulf states implies that these states can be dealt with as a bloc and that the GCC is an effective enough organization to be dealt with as if it were the equivalent of NATO. He adds, "One of the key challenges the U.S. faces in the southern Gulf is that there are strong rivalries and differences in strategic interests between the individual southern Gulf states, and that the GCC is almost totally ineffective in achieving regional cooperation and is likely to remain so. U.S. relations with Bahrain, Kuwait, Oman, Qatar, Saudi Arabia, and the U.A.E. must be tailored to different national needs, and conducted largely on a bilateral basis."

[3] John Duke Anthony opines that the same can be said of having been true as a result of U.S. forces in NATO countries (e.g., Greece, Italy, Spain, Turkey, et al.), and over a far longer period, with substantially greater overall numbers than the United States has deployed inside the GCC countries. Yet the criticism was never so great as to cause the United States to cut and run, nor did it (as in Libya) result in any premature eviction or drawdown of the forces employed.

new challenges in the decade ahead posed by the population explosion and constraints on their economic and social programs, particularly given the prediction of only a slow rise in their oil revenues.

To consider these problems, the Council on Foreign Relations asked a group of distinguished American experts in Gulf affairs to study current U.S. policies and recommend possible modifications that, in close consultation with U.S. allies, would allow the United States to pursue its objectives of Gulf security and stability more effectively.

This Statement and the accompanying Report are the result.

RECOMMENDATIONS

The Study Group recommends that the U.S. government reassess its policy in the following nine areas:

1. *General U.S. Gulf Policy*
The Gulf region requires a focus distinct from the Arab-Israeli peace process. While peace process issues and Gulf policies are linked in many ways, any review of or modification to current Gulf policy should not be hostage to the achievement of a comprehensive peace between Israel and its front-line neighbors.

2. *Iraq*
While U.S. policy has kept Saddam Hussein's government weak and Iraq's program for WMD under tight control, the continued effectiveness of this policy is under challenge. Dual containment was never meant to be a long-term solution. Humanitarian concerns, the disintegration of Iraqi society, and continued division within the Kurdish movements in northern Iraq trouble U.S. allies and may undermine support for U.S. strategy in the United States as well as the Gulf. A more humane alternative would involve continuing provision of humanitarian relief under U.N. Security Council Resolution 986 combined with more focused military pressure on targets of value to Saddam Hussein. Furthermore, America's expectations of Iraq must become more specific, and the United States should

consider whether economic sanctions should be narrowed, to maintain U.S. cooperation with key members of the international coalition in the Gulf, particularly Britain, France, and Turkey. In the meantime, the United States should maintain its capability to defend Kuwait and sustain no-fly and no-air-defense zones in southern Iraq. However, the United States must take into account that some American Gulf allies are more concerned with the growing strength of neighboring Iran and worry less about what Saddam Hussein will do if he remains in power. *Accordingly:*

a. The United States should restate its commitment to the territorial integrity of Iraq and the human rights of all Iraqis, while continuing to oppose Saddam Hussein's leadership.

b. If the collapse of the regime in Iraq is the only acceptable outcome for the United States, then the United States should openly assert that it will not under any circumstances deal with the regime of Saddam Hussein. Such a statement might provide an additional incentive for internal change in Iraq. As a corollary, Washington must accept that change will most likely come from the inner circles of the military or the Ba'ath party. The United States should declare ahead of time its willingness to deal with any new Iraqi government that accepts U.N. resolutions and international norms, including ones on respecting Kuwaiti independence and on negotiated settlements of the problem of Kuwaiti prisoners of war. If any new government accedes to these conditions, the United States should be prepared to move quickly to deal with this leadership, likely weaker than the current government which has had a quarter-century to entrench itself in power. The possibility of relief from claims of war reparations as a reward for new leadership should also be discussed with countries holding claims. Current U.S. signals may give the impression that if a new government in Iraq comes from within the existing power structure, it would be treated the same way the government of Saddam Hussein is being treated—thereby reducing potential opponents' incentives to act.[4]

---

[4] Secretary of State Madeleine Albright moved the American position closer to this recommendation in her remarks "Preserving Principle and Safeguarding Stability: U.S.

c. The unpleasant reality may be however, that Saddam remains in power indefinitely. The United States needs to formulate and articulate a coherent policy toward Iraq for this eventuality. The United States must also do what it can to lessen the fragmentation of Iraqi society. A healthy society will be needed to make a post-Saddam Iraq viable and will also encourage opposition forces against Saddam Hussein.

3. Iran

America lacks a clear end game, seems unconcerned with Iranian energy exports, and is experiencing policy tensions with its allies. Washington acknowledges it has not changed Iranian behavior on the issues of terrorism, acquisition of weapons of mass destruction, or opposition to Arab-Israeli peace.[5] The Study Group affirms that military containment of Iran must continue. In addition, it suggests that the U.S. government should consider tests to Iran's adherence to international norms and offer incentives to achieve these changes.[6] The United States should begin with *modest steps:*

a. Reduce the intensity of the rhetorical war, which gives Iran the impression that the United States seeks nothing less than the demise of its government. In turn, state that Washington expects a reciprocal toning down of Iranian rhetoric vis-à-vis the United States and its allies.

Policy Toward Iraq," at Georgetown University, March 26, 1997. But she stopped short of explicitly stating that the United States will never deal with Saddam Hussein.

[5] Cordesman disagrees. U.S. pressure and sanctions have confronted Iran with very serious problems in importing arms and dual-use technology for its weapons of mass destruction. Iran's military build-up and arms imports are a fraction of the level Iran planned in the early 1990s, and Iran is experiencing continuing problems in obtaining technology and material for biological, chemical, and nuclear weapons. U.S. policy has restricted Iran's freedom of action in its use of terrorism and has had a considerable impact in leading Europe to be cautious in its relations with Iran and in pushing our allies to maintain the "critical" in critical dialogue.

[6] James A. Placke believes that the outcome of the Mykonos trial presents both the justification and opportunity to attract the support of America's principal allies for more intensive isolation of the present Iranian regime. Robin Wright posits that the trial presents the justification and opening for joint action with our European allies in a number of ways.

b. Reduce the economic embargo to a narrow range of specific items such as WMD components, missiles, and dual-use technology.[7]

c. Encourage the International Atomic Energy Agency (IAEA) to carry out a more aggressive program of inspections.[8]

d. Explore the potential of dialogue through track-two channels to Iran.

4. Force Restructuring

So long as tensions with Iran and Iraq remain, some American forces will be needed in the region. American forces are an effective deterrent against conventional threats and their presence helps GCC leaders face down criticisms from Baghdad and Tehran about their support for the Arab-Israeli peace. However, the troops' presence also feeds domestic dissent.

While American forces will remain in the region for the foreseeable future, current levels of U.S. forces and their configuration should be reexamined. It may be possible to reduce the visible aspects of the U.S. presence without reducing U.S. ability to project substantial military power in the Gulf.[9] Even before devising

---

[7] Gary G. Sick observes: "The lifting of some existing sanctions could serve as a positive inducement to secure improved Iranian cooperation in the WMD area." He also states that while the United States should maintain pressure on Iran in certain areas, it should be prepared to acknowledge and encourage moderate Iranian policies in other areas, such as Central Asia and Afghanistan. The United States should also be prepared to consult, directly or indirectly, on issues such as Iraq, where Iran has legitimate security interests and concerns.

[8] Cordesman points out that the "IAEA can only inspect declared nuclear facilities, and its normal method of inspection is limited largely to nuclear fuel cycle activities. The Study Group does not address the core issue of nuclear proliferation unless Iran agrees to vastly increase the scope of IAEA freedom of action, the IAEA organizes to conduct the same kind of intrusive surprise inspection it might use in Iraq, and/or Iran moves far enough along in the fuel cycle for reactor inspection to provide reliable results (assuming that the reactor design does not include a concealed irradiation chamber). There is a serious risk, in fact, that the IAEA inspections will simply appear to 'clear' Iran and legitimate its nuclear programs as 'peaceful.' Further, Iran has extensive chemical weapons, and the CIA reports that it has begun to deploy biological weapons. Iran must now be approaching a level of biotechnology where such weapons can be as lethal as tactical weapons. Accordingly, the Study Group recommendation may do more harm than good."

[9] Dov S. Zakheim adds that many of the Study Group's concerns about American presence (other than the problem of long deployments) could be ameliorated by a more

a more sustainable and affordable long-term strategy, the United States should reduce the forces to the minimum necessary and lessen their attraction as a target by:

a. Carrying out an internal reassessment of the future of the forces in northern Saudi Arabia used to enforce the no-fly zone. Even if these forces might play a role in defending against an Iraqi invasion of GCC states, we must question whether the present configuration is essential.

b. Making publicly clear that most of the U.S. Air Force presence in Saudi Arabia is temporary and aimed at enforcing the no-fly zone in southern Iraq,[10] and linking this to an American intention to reduce these forces after the emergence of a government in Iraq that accepts and implements U.N. resolutions.

c. Although conventional military threats to oil market stability require a strategic response, including a U.S. military presence, long-term U.S. strategy must include maintaining some balance of power between Iran and Iraq. There is no other state or combination of states in the Gulf capable of matching Iran's and Iraq's power.[11]

5. Arab-Israeli Peace

The United States must continue its intensive efforts to achieve a comprehensive Arab-Israeli peace. A strong relationship exists between progress on that front and area-wide cooperation with the United States.

---

maritime-oriented presence. Carrier-based tactical aviation, coupled with a maritime presence, could maintain both a credible deterrent and sustain the no-fly zones, at least in southern Iraq.

[10] Cordesman states that the reality is that close cooperation between the United States and Saudi air forces is critical to our war fighting capability in dealing with both Iraq and Iran, and that some form of U.S. air presence will be required indefinitely into the future. There should be no "cut and run" approach that will create more problems than it will solve, will encourage further attacks on U.S. forces throughout the Gulf, and will seriously undermine U.S. national interests.

[11] Cordesman finds that "there is no present need for a U.S. strategy to maintain a balance of power between Iran and Iraq. Iran and Iraq will have sufficient military strength to counterbalance each other indefinitely without U.S. intervention, and the need for intervention in the long-term balance will be highly dependent on the character of each regime and the specific military conditions at the time. The United States does have a strategic interest in strengthening the military forces of the southern Gulf states relative to both Iran and Iraq."

6. Burden Sharing

The United States should devise and implement a long-term strategy that relies less on the military budget and maintains public support for the U.S. deployment. Thus it should:

a. Negotiate larger financial contributions to support the U.S. military presence in the Gulf from the European countries and Japan.[12]

b. Educate Congress and the American public as to why the U.S. role as security guarantor in the Gulf will continue to be necessary.

7. Consultation

The United States must consult with both the GCC states and Israel on matters of policy toward the Gulf. We believe that Washington has not been sufficiently attentive to the need of pursuing close and frequent consultation about its Gulf policies with members of the GCC. To the extent that internal threats to security exist in GCC states and are not identical within each state, and to the extent that the states' attitudes differ even on issues of external security, it is essential that the United States consult with each state individually, and regularly, over the implementation of its policy in the Gulf.[13] Moreover, since developments in the Gulf, especially developing Iranian and Iraqi capabilities in weapons of mass destruction, affect Israeli security, the United States must regularly consult with Israel on matters of Gulf policy.

---

[12] Cordesman thinks that "there is little real-world prospect that our European allies and Japan will assume added burden sharing to maintain day-to-day U.S. capabilities, nor should they. This recommendation ignores the fact that U.S. defense spending will soon be roughly the same burden as a percent of our total GDP (2.7 percent) and federal budget (14 percent) as during the isolationist era at the end of the Great Depression. It costs money to be a superpower. There may be a case for trying to negotiate additional contributions in the case of a major build-up or significant regional conflict."

[13] Michael H. Van Dusen qualifies his support for this point. Consultation on security issues with GCC states is extensive. Because the United States has a large military presence and many military assets in the region, visits to the area by U.S. military leaders are numerous. What is needed is more high-level U.S. diplomatic and political attention to complement what is done on the military side.

8. Promotion of Long-Term U.S. Commercial and Energy Interests

Given that Iran and a post-Saddam Iraq are major states that will eventually be re-integrated into the international community, it is important for long-term U.S. economic and strategic interests that American business not be kept at a significant disadvantage in international competition. The United States should follow the example of some European countries in allowing U.S. companies to negotiate deals with Iran and a post-Saddam Iraq, on the understanding that these cannot be implemented until after the sanctions are removed.[14]

9. Political Participation

The United States has enjoyed close and mutually beneficial relations with the states of the GCC and their leadership for many years. It should do nothing even to imply a distancing from its security responsibilities as these leaders cope with the challenges of a new generation's expectations and a changed economic environment.

Internal economic and political challenges will confront the leadership of the GCC states with choices, either in the direction of further limiting political participation or that of more economic and political liberalization. Long-term American interests are better served by encouraging the latter. The United States must proceed with sensitivity and respect for these long-term friends and allies, and acknowledge that it cannot devise specific reform strategies but can still encourage reform through *modest steps:*

---

[14] According to Cordesman, the Study Group should have specifically addressed Iranian and Iraqi energy production and exports, and the gap between a U.S. policy of sanctions and dual containment and U.S. Department of Energy projections of massive increases in Iranian and Iraqi oil production. Iran has some 67–90 billion barrels of oil reserves (roughly 10 percent of total world reserves) and 620–741 trillion cubic feet of gas. This inevitably makes it increasingly critical to the world's oil supplies. Furthermore, the difference between energy security issues and military security issues should be addressed by U.S. policymakers. It may be possible to specify kinds of investment that do not provide Iran with sudden increases in cash flow which could affect its military spending, and to allow investment in Iraq under the same kinds of constraints enforced by U.N. Security Council Resolution 986. On the same point, Sick notes that increasing global demand for supplies of oil and gas in the 21st century will require additional production capacity in the Gulf and elsewhere. U.S. policy should promote, not obstruct, normal development of non-nuclear energy resources.

a. Encourage gradual political reform through the enhancement of the role of consultative councils in the GCC states and the parliament in Kuwait to address structural economic and political issues. The councils are consultative, not legislative, and members tend to be chosen by the rulers. The current structure of these councils makes them more useful for addressing personal grievances than broader political and economic problems.

b. Emphasize the need for economic reform, especially privatization of the economy. In particular, encourage GCC states to foster a climate that attracts more foreign investment—an essential step for economic growth. Foreign investors will, in turn, demand an environment of transparency and accountability.

c. Elevate the issues of political and economic reform on the agenda of discussions with Gulf leaders, emphasizing the mutuality of long-term interest on these issues. The United States must stress that the economic future of the region will be difficult if current population trends remain unchecked.

MEMBERS OF THE INDEPENDENT STUDY GROUP

RICHARD W. MURPHY, Chair of the Study Group, is the Hasib J. Sabbagh Senior Fellow for the Middle East at the Council on Foreign Relations. He was the Assistant Secretary of State for Near Eastern and South Asian Affairs from 1983 to 1989.

JOHN DUKE ANTHONY† is President and Chief Executive Officer of the National Council on U.S.-Arab Relations. For more than two decades, he has been a consultant to the Departments of Defense and State on the Arabian Peninsula and the Gulf States.

BEN L. BONK* is the National Intelligence Officer for the Near East and South Asia.

ANTHONY H. CORDESMAN† is Co-Director of the Middle East Program at the Center for Strategic and International Studies and Director of the Gulf Net Assessment Project.

MICHELE DUROCHER DUNNE* is a member of the Policy Planning Staff, U.S. Department of State. She has served on the National Intelligence Council and the State Department's Bureau of Intelligence and Research, and at the U.S. Consulate General in Jerusalem.

CHARLES W. FREEMAN, JR., is Chairman of Projects International, Inc. He was Assistant Secretary of Defense for International Security Affairs and U.S. Ambassador to Saudi Arabia during the Gulf War.

---

*Individual participated in the Study Group discussions but was not asked to endorse the Statement or Recommendations because of his or her official capacity.

†Individual largely concurs with the Statement and Recommendations but has endorsed one or more footnotes.

Note: Institutional affiliations listed for identification purposes only.

RICHARD K. HERRMANN is Associate Professor of Political Science and Associate Director of the Mershon Center for International Security at Ohio State University.

JOSEPH P. HOAR is President of J.P. Hoar and Associates and was the Commander in Chief of the U. S. Central Command. He is also Chairman of the Middle East Forum of the Council on Foreign Relations.

JUDITH KIPPER is Director of the Middle East Forum of the Council on Foreign Relations and Co-Director of the Middle East Studies Program at the Center for Strategic and International Studies. She is also a consultant for ABC News.

ELLEN LAIPSON* is Special Assistant to the U.S. Ambassador to the United Nations. She worked on Gulf issues at the National Security Council from 1993 to 1995.

ROBERT LITWAK is Director of International Studies at the Woodrow Wilson Center. He served as Director for Nonproliferation and Export Controls at the National Security Council.

PHEBE A. MARR is a Senior Fellow at the Institute for National Strategic Studies, National Defense University. She is a scholar of the modern history of Iraq and Gulf politics.

THOMAS L. MCNAUGHER is Associate Director of the Arroyo Center at the RAND Corporation. He is the author of *Arms and Oil: U.S. Military Strategy and the Persian Gulf* (Washington, D.C.: The Brookings Insitution, 1985).

GEORGE CRANWELL MONTGOMERY is a partner in the Washington office of Baker, Donelson, Bearman & Caldwell. He was Ambassador to the Sultanate of Oman and served as Counsel to the Majority Leader of the U.S. Senate.

---

*Individual participated in the Study Group discussions but was not asked to endorse the Statement or Recommendations because of his or her official capacity.

†Individual largely concurs with the Statement and Recommendations but has endorsed one or more footnotes.

Note: Institutional affiliations listed for identification purposes only.

JAMES A. PLACKE† is Director for Middle East Research at Cambridge Energy Research Associates. He previously served at a number of U.S. embassies in the Middle East and North Africa and as a Deputy Assistant Secretary of State for Near Eastern Affairs.

GARY G. SICK† is a Senior Research Scholar at Columbia University and the Executive Director of the Gulf 2000 research project. He was a member of the National Security Council from 1976 to 1981 with special responsibility for Persian Gulf affairs.

HENRY SIEGMAN is Senior Fellow on the Middle East and Director of the U.S./Middle East Project at the Council on Foreign Relations. He was formerly National Executive Director of the American Jewish Congress.

SHIBLEY TELHAMI is Associate Professor of Government and Director of the Program for Contemporary Near Eastern Studies at Cornell University. He is also a Non-Resident Fellow at the Brookings Institution.

MICHAEL H. VAN DUSEN† is the Democratic Chief of Staff on the Committee on International Relations of the U.S. House of Representatives. He has served with the Committee for over 25 years.

ROBIN WRIGHT† is the author of two books on Iran and is a former Mideast correspondent for *The Sunday Times* of London. She now covers global trends for *The Los Angeles Times*.

MONA YACOUBIAN* is a Middle East analyst at the State Department. In 1995–96, she was an International Affairs Fellow at the Council on Foreign Relations.

---

*Individual participated in the Study Group discussions but was not asked to endorse the Statement or Recommendations because of his or her official capacity.
†Individual largely concurs with the Statement and Recommendations but has endorsed one or more footnotes.
Note: Institutional affiliations listed for identification purposes only.

Dov S. Zakheim† is Chief Executive Officer of SPC International Corporation of Arlington, Virginia. He is a former Deputy Under Secretary of Defense for Planning and Resources.

Vahan Zanoyan is the President and CEO of the Petroleum Finance Company. He has served as a consultant on the commercial and strategic aspects of the global oil and gas business to private and governmental organizations worldwide.

Rapporteur

Nomi Colton-Max is Program Associate for the Middle East at the Council on Foreign Relations. She received an M.A. in international relations and economics from the Johns Hopkins School of Advanced International Studies.

---

*Individual participated in the Study Group discussions but was not asked to endorse the Statement or Recommendations because of his or her official capacity.

†Individual largely concurs with the Statement and Recommendations but has endorsed one or more footnotes.

Note: Institutional affiliations listed for identification purposes only.

BACKGROUND REPORT OF THE INDEPENDENT STUDY GROUP

Access to Gulf oil at reasonable prices was identified as a vital U.S. interest in the Nixon administration, but American concern for security and stability in the Persian Gulf region has steadily increased since World War II. The United States now views assuring security and stability in the area as its global duty. Some American observers assume that the United States has no choice in the Gulf and that it will be able to play its present role indefinitely. The Study Group challenges this assumption and explains why a careful reassessment of current policy and the means available to secure American interests in the Gulf are necessary.

Washington formally succeeded London as the primary guarantor of Gulf security in 1971 but was not called on for military action until 1987. In the 1970s, the United States relied primarily on the shah's Iran to balance power in the region. With the overthrow of the shah in 1979, Washington was forced to rethink its strategy. During the Iran-Iraq war that started one year later, the United States shifted its support back and forth between the two, while continuing to strengthen Saudi Arabia. The Iraqi invasion of Kuwait in 1990 once again brought an end to this type of thinking. Under the Clinton administration's policy of dual containment, Washington has worked to isolate Iraq and Iran, to block their acquisition of weapons of mass destruction, and prevent them from engaging in terrorism and subversion. This policy of isolation, while a reasonable stopgap in the wake of the Gulf War, does not provide an adequate basis for long-term security and stability in the region.

THE CURRENT INITIATIVE

The United States has maintained a naval command in Bahrain for the past half-century and a military training mission in Saudi Arabia for almost as long, and has offered training opportunities to the other Arab Gulf states as well. It sold these states increasingly sophisticated military equipment. The six Arab Gulf states—Saudi Arabia, Kuwait, Bahrain, Qatar, the United Arab Emirates and Oman—established the Gulf Cooperation Council (GCC) in 1981 to improve coordination and better assure mutual security.

The Clinton administration, like every administration since Nixon, has publicly restated the position that the United States has vital interests in the Gulf. U.S. military strategy since the Pentagon's "Bottom-Up Review" of September 1993, which assessed U.S. defense needs in the post–Cold War era, has focused on maintaining the capability to fight two simultaneous regional wars, one them in the Gulf.[1] Military planning, weapons procurement, and training are influenced by the possibility that the United States will fight a major war in the Persian Gulf.

Since the invasion of Kuwait, U.S. policy in the Gulf has focused on four objectives: assuring access to oil at reasonable prices, supporting GCC states against regional threats emanating from Iraq and Iran, preventing the proliferation of weapons of mass destruction, and minimizing the threat of terrorism. The United States has been committed to the implementation of U.N. resolutions on Iraq. It has also asserted that a less authoritarian and more representative Iraqi government is an important American interest. Finally, the United States has continued to see the goal of attaining a just, durable, and comprehensive Arab-Israeli peace to be of central importance to American policy, and has sought to isolate states opposed to that peace.

In recent years the central instrument of American policy in the Gulf has been its military forces, present today in several GCC states and afloat in the Gulf. These forces are organized to support friendly states, deter potential adversaries, and, if necessary, fight to win against an aggressor. The enforcement of applicable U.N. Security Council resolutions and of the "no-fly zone" in southern Iraq, along with the deterrence of Iranian aggression are the primary

---

[1] The Pentagon is currently drafting its quadrennial defense review for submission to Congress in May 1997. The two-conflict approach is expected to be retained in this review.

goals. Forces for these tasks are largely naval, except for the air force wing stationed in Saudi Arabia. An extensive joint exercise program deploys units stationed in the United States to the region for limited periods.

U.S. military strategy has been successful in deterring Iraqi and Iranian conventional threats, although it has been unable to deter Saddam Hussein from using his forces against his own people in Iraq. GCC fears stemming from the Iraqi invasion of Kuwait, combined with early U.S. successes in engineering progress in Arab-Israeli peace, eased GCC acceptance of the deployment of U.S. forces in the region. The deployment has greatly increased Washington's ability to deter hostile acts and quickly mobilize forces and equipment in the region as needed. Since the war, the United States has enhanced its naval presence in the region, positioned equipment for elements of two armed brigades in Kuwait and Qatar, and maintained a wing of combat aircraft in Saudi Arabia to enforce the no-fly zone in southern Iraq. The United States has also benefited from Turkey's permission to temporarily station additional American forces on its soil to carry out "Operation Provide Comfort" in northern Iraq. In addition, the United States is currently expanding American capabilities by establishing a division base set in the Gulf region. These deployments have helped deter Iraqi and Iranian conventional threats, and enabled the United States to respond rapidly as in October 1994 when Iraqi troop movements again threatened Kuwait. However, the events in northern Iraq in August 1996, when Saddam Hussein helped one Kurdish leader against another, showed that the Iraqi leader still has the military capability to seriously embarrass American policymakers.

Although labeling both Iraq and Iran "rogue regimes," the United States has, in principle, differentiated between them. The U.S. government has found it impossible to reconcile itself to the existing Iraqi government and has tacitly sought its demise.[2] Meanwhile, American policy makers have stated that "more normal relations with Iran are conceivable," although acknowledging that reconciliation

---

[2] In a March 26, 1997, speech on Iraq, Secretary of State Madeleine Albright virtually ruled out any dealings with Saddam Hussein's regime.

will be difficult.[3] But the U.S. believes that the choice is Iran's and that American incentives are not warranted in the meantime. In 1996, however, House Speaker Newt Gingrich's call to undermine the Iranian government and President Clinton's signing of the Iran and Libya Sanctions Act, which punishes foreign companies that invest more than $40 million in Iran's (or Libya's) energy sector, have blurred the distinction between Iran and Iraq in U.S. policy.

While U.S. policy has deterred external threats to GCC states and protected the supply of oil, it has not as yet fully achieved its goals. In Iran, despite the escalation of sanctions over the past two years, the American government asserts that Tehran has continued its sponsorship of terrorism and subversion, its efforts to acquire weapons of mass destruction, and its strident opposition to the Arab-Israeli peace process. In Iraq, the government that ordered the invasion of Kuwait remains entrenched in Baghdad and has extended its influence in northern Iraq. Generally speaking, the Gulf War coalition remains supportive of the primary objective of implementing U.N. resolutions, but has serious concerns about the increasing economic and political costs of current policies. U.S. policies toward Iraq, which were adopted in 1990–91, are causing friction with Turkey, the European allies, Japan, some of the GCC states, and, to a lesser degree, the Iraqi Kurds, some of whom have found it in their interest to cooperate with the Iraqi government. The coalition's reluctance to endorse the use of Cruise missiles against Iraq in September 1996 signaled increasing strain. The GCC states worry that current policies may produce the undesirable consequence of Iraq's fragmentation. Provision of humanitarian relief under U.N. Security Council Resolution 986 may partially satisfy American allies, but even if Washington can maintain sanctions against Iraq indefinitely, humanitarian considerations make continuation of the status quo costly for the

---

[3] Anthony Lake, "Confronting Backlash States" in *Foreign Affairs*, March 1994, pp. 45–55. Last year, Assistant Secretary of State Robert H. Pelletreau, Jr., said: "We remain ready for an authorized, out-in-the-open dialogue when Iran's leaders are willing to discuss our differences face-to-face. There is no hidden agenda. Iran has never indicated an interest in such a dialogue however. We are ready to welcome Iran's return to the international community when it demonstrates that it is prepared to live by the same basic rules and international standards that other states do" (in a speech at the Council on Foreign Relations, May 8, 1996).

United States. We must fear the prospect of Iraq becoming a Humpty Dumpty that will be impossible to put back together.

Furthermore, current military strategy may prove too costly for both the United States and the GCC states to sustain over the long term. In 1995 and 1996, American troops were twice attacked in Saudi Arabia. As for the GCC states, the prevalent assumption is that they are rich, when in fact they are getting poorer. Saudi Arabia's average per capita income, for example, has declined by more than half in the past decade. Once states with enviable financial reserves, today Kuwait and Saudi Arabia have substantial domestic public debt. GCC states paid a high price to expel Iraq from Kuwait, and continue to pay hundreds of millions of dollars a year for the U.S. presence, in addition to their own substantial defense budgets. Unexpected costs have also been incurred, and not just because of external threats such as the 1994 Iraqi moves southward. The bombings against U.S. troops in Dhahran, for example, caused Washington to reposition American forces in Saudi Arabia, increasing the price of U.S. involvement.

The aggregate cost to the one-dimensional economies of the GCC states has raised concern in the region about the long-term effects of military expenditure on societies that sorely need to expand their physical and social infrastructure. This is especially troubling given the economic projections that show oil income is not likely to rise substantially for GCC states. Unemployment is an increasing problem, massive investments are needed to expand production capacities, and populations are increasing at the rate of 3.0–3.5 percent annually. This demographic explosion is a threat to the long-term economic and social well-being, and thus the stability, of the GCC states.

Washington's policies prevent American business from competing in Iran and Iraq. The human costs of the current American strategy are steep as well. Since only a few hundred service personnel and their families are permanently assigned in the region, personnel are assigned on a temporary basis, with most troops serving for three to six months away from home stations. Some personnel can expect to be away from home over 200 days a year. These deployments are often repetitive and take a toll on the troops because of their temporary nature, the harsh climate in the Gulf region, and the isolation that comes from living in a foreign culture. The burden is further increased since some military organizations have contingency commitments in as many as three theaters of operation.

While the Clinton administration's call to contain Iran and Iraq is continuing, international resolve to isolate the two countries is weakening. This trend is not surprising. Both states are important regional powers with significant strategic capabilities and important oil and gas resources for world energy supplies that make them hard to ignore. The bitter European reaction to the Iran and Libya Sanctions Act, the $23 billion gas deal between Turkey and Iran, and the difficulty the United States had in persuading Turkey in late 1996 to extend permission for the presence of U.S. forces needed for Operation Northern Watch, are measures of other countries' uneasiness with American policy.

U.S. efforts to improve the general efficiency of the armed forces of the GCC states and encouragement of expensive equipment sales have enabled opposition groups to exploit existing anti-Western sentiment by underscoring the negative aspects of the U.S. presence. They argue that this presence undermines the sovereignty of the GCC states. Attacks on American troops in Saudi Arabia in 1995 and 1996 and continued unrest in Bahrain suggest that there are internal threats in the region that U.S. military strategy has only indirectly addressed.

The conflict between Israel and Arab parties has often caused tension between two American priorities: Western access to Gulf oil at reasonable prices and commitment to the survival and security of the state of Israel. For even though the American commitment to the Gulf region has never wavered, at times the U.S. role in this area has been seen as subsidiary to its role in the Levant and the Arab-Israeli peace process. In recent years, the Gulf's reaction to the Iraqi invasion of Kuwait and U.S. identification with forward movement in the peace process have helped reduce, but have not entirely eliminated, the tension between these two objectives.

Setbacks in the peace process following the 1996 Israeli elections have stimulated greater interest in several Arab capitals in bringing Iraq back into the Arab community. With the recent change of government in Jordan, Amman may be repairing its ties with Baghdad; Egypt is urging the return of Iraq to the Arab fold; and the lower Gulf states are initiating dialogue with Iraq. Furthermore, continued conflict between Kurdish groups in northern Iraq is pushing the new government in Turkey to rethink its policy toward Iraq.

THE NATURE OF AMERICAN INTERESTS
IN THE PERSIAN GULF

1. Energy

Holding more that two-thirds of the world's current known oil reserves, the Persian Gulf region is strategically important for the United States. Early in the Cold War, American interest in the area stemmed from the fear that these valuable oil resources might fall into the hands of the Soviet Union. American strategy consequently focused on deterring the Soviet threat and defending the region against this threat. Events over the next 40 years were shaped by this concern and were also affected by the changing relations between oil-producing countries and the United States. The oil shocks of 1973 and 1979 illustrated American reliance on this resource and reinforced America's commitment to its vital interests in the region. The end of the Cold War eliminated further concerns about Soviet designs on the region. But the Iraqi invasion of Kuwait bolstered Washington's worries over Iranian and Iraqi challenges to the GCC states, which had preoccupied the United States in the Iraqi case since 1961 and in Iran's since the 1979 revolution.

While dealing with these challenges, the following factors about energy and the way that it affects American interests in the region must be kept in mind:

- All Gulf oil suppliers, including Iran and Iran, will continue to rely heavily on their oil income. Oil-producing states vary in their view of oil markets. Some, particularly Iraq and Iran, have relished the periodic price spikes of the past more than Saudi Arabia, which has preferred long-term market stability.

[39]

- *Long-term* energy prices are determined more by market factors than by military strategy.

- Short-term disruptions in market stability are likely to continue to be caused by internal instability and threats from Iraq or Iran, especially if directed against Saudi Arabia.

- The recent return of Iraqi oil to the market has been reflected in the short-term price drop at the start of 1997. Oil prices are expected to remain relatively flat, and the region's real export revenues per capita are expected to be less than half those achieved during the boom years of 1975–82.

- The structure of the oil industry is changing because of technological innovation, resource availability, and competition. These dynamics should yield relative long-term oil price stability, despite growing consumption. Gains in technology are substantially reducing the cost of development and production. Consequently, the difference in the cost of oil produced by the GCC states and the non-GCC producers is declining.

- Current predictions for world production capacity of oil are much higher than estimates of a decade ago, and the Gulf's portion of this capacity will be smaller than had been expected.

- As for the United States, Saudi Arabia is no longer its primary crude oil supplier. It has been surpassed by Venezuela, and is being overtaken by Canada and Mexico. Transportation and inventory-storage costs are the key factors in this shift.

- East Asian demand for energy will have an increasing impact on the future of the world oil market. Economic development in India and China alone is likely to affect Asian oil demands significantly, sparking a dramatic increase. Average annual growth of Pacific Rim consumption for 1994–2015 is projected to be 4.6 percent; the projected rate for China is 2.6 percent.[4] Today coal is the pri-

---

[4] Energy Information Agency, *Annual Energy Outlook with Projections to 2015* (Washington, D.C.: Department of Energy, 1996), pp. 178–80. The Pacific Rim refers to Hong Kong, Malaysia, Singapore, South Korea, Taiwan, and Thailand. The figure for the Pacific Rim (4.6 percent) is double every other world grouping except for China.

mary energy provider in East Asia, but dramatic economic growth, industrialization, investment, and environmental concerns will certainly enlarge the demand for energy.

• Gulf oil represents only 8.5 percent of U.S. consumption but 23 percent of Europe's and nearly 70 percent of Japan's.[5] Globally, Europe and Japan are also much more dependent on oil imports than the United States.

• The world oil market is an integrated one, and price disruptions in one area ripple immediately through the system. This by no means diminishes U.S. interests in oil and the Gulf. When the United States imported globally even less oil in 1973, it still suffered all the inflation and economic dislocation generated by the Arab oil boycott of that year. The Gulf remains important because it is the world's "swing producer" of oil. It has 65 percent of the world's known oil reserves and at least four million barrels a day in excess production capacity. In today's market that may not matter too much, but if supply or demand tightens in the future, events and decisions in the Gulf would affect the price of oil more than events and decisions elsewhere.

2. Limiting the Spread of Weapons of Mass Destruction
The United States will continue to place great importance on slowing the proliferation of weapons of mass destruction in general, and the growth of Iraqi and Iranian capabilities in particular. The United Nations Special Commission on Iraq (UNSCOM) has done outstanding work in investigating and destroying Iraqi weapons of mass destruction. The issue of WMD, however, involves other states in the region, including Syria, Egypt, Libya, and Israel. Further work on WMD will ultimately require a broader regional effort. This is unlikely to succeed so long as Iran and Iraq remain isolated. Similarly, only with significant progress in the Arab-Israeli process will serious attempts to curtail the proliferation of WMD be accepted in the region.

---

[5] Figures from 1996 in "The International Petroleum Statistics Report" (Washington, D.C.: Energy Information Administration, Office of Energy Markets and End Use, U.S. Department of Energy, January 1997).

Such proliferation depends in part on the availability of supplies on the international market, and the United States has focused much of its efforts on limiting Iraqi and Iranian access to that market. However, the prohibitive cost of conventional military capability for states like Iran and Iraq has sharpened their desire to acquire cheaper non-conventional arms to counter U.S. power. Military and economic containment of the two states will probably require diplomacy directed toward providing them with incentives to discourage WMD, and creating regionwide regimes to regulate these weapons.

In early 1995 Israel informed Egypt of its readiness to discuss the establishment of a zone free from WMD two years after the establishment of a comprehensive and durable peace in the area. The proposal contained the provision that peace must include the achievement of bilateral peace agreements between Israel and all Arab League members, plus Iran. Egypt reportedly considered this provision unacceptable, arguing that Israel should limit its insistence on bilateral peace agreements to the "front-line" Arab states of Jordan, Syria and Lebanon. This, nonetheless, represented a change in Israel's stance from its earlier declaration that "it would not be the first to employ nuclear weapons in the area."

3. Fighting Terrorism and Subversion

Terrorism remains a threat to the stability of states in the Persian Gulf and to U.S. personnel and interests. Unlike conventional warfare, terrorism is relatively inexpensive to carry out, vitiating the assumption that economic sanctions will reduce its occurrence. Washington has asserted that Iran's sponsorship of terrorism has increased, despite escalation of U.S. economic sanctions on Iran in the past few years. Yet while this sponsorship continues, much of the terrorism facing the GCC states and the Arab world has domestic roots. If so, the problem cannot be addressed simply by military means or by the economic and political containment of Iran and Iraq.

While the United States can inflict much economic damage on the two countries, and Iranian and Iraqi forces are no match for their American counterparts, escalating the confrontation could lead to increased subversion within GCC states. It is clear, for example, that the disadvantaged Shi'ite majority in Bahrain has close religious and cultural links with Iran that Iran has exploited. Similarly, the smaller GCC states, which have large populations of foreign workers, are vulnerable to subversion. Although there is little evidence for such activity, the potential for terrorism concerns GCC leaders. In the United Arab Emirates, for example, foreign workers constituted 75 percent of the population in 1995. Abu Dhabi is uneasy about the possibility for subversive action among the many Iranian workers on U.A.E. territory. Complicating responses to subversive and terrorist threats is the difficult task of identifying the perpetrators, especially when there are no claims of responsibility.

4. Arab-Israeli Peace

The U.S. commitment to Israeli security is a central component of U.S. policy. Peace and security in the Gulf would be strengthened by a comprehensive Arab-Israeli peace. In fact, security in both subregions is a prerequisite for peace because Arab-Israeli peace will not be assured if established only with the front-line states of Egypt, Jordan, Syria, and Lebanon. Fear of nonconventional threats to Israel from Iraq and Iran affects those formulating U.S. policy for the region. There can be no regional disarmament or long-run economic integration until this broader security is achieved.

Since the 1993 Oslo accords between Israel and the Palestine Liberation Organization, the Arab Gulf states have assumed that Arab-Israeli peace is achievable. However, the 1995 Alexandria Summit between Egypt, Syria, and Saudi Arabia sent a cautionary message to the smaller Gulf states that they should await further progress on the Syrian-Israeli track before normalizing their own relations with Israel. The delays in the peace process following the 1996 Israeli elections revived serious concerns within the GCC states, reflecting both fear of regional instability and popular concern for the plight of the Palestinian people. The goodwill that Prime Minister Benjamin Netanyahu garnered with the signing of the Hebron Protocol in January 1997 was depleted when he launched the Har Homa-Abu Ghneim settlement project in East Jerusalem. GCC leaders will closely monitor the way the Netanyahu government proceeds.

THE U.S. MILITARY STRATEGY FOR ACHIEVING
U.S. POLITICAL OBJECTIVES

The Pentagon's strategic approach is "one of engagement, forward presence, and rapid response" that centers on "the maintenance and enhancement of our ability to protect our interest through military force."[6] The aims of the strategy are, first, to deter aggression, and second, should deterrence fail, to provide the capability to apply decisive force. Iran and Iraq are seen as the two likely aggressors. The Department of Defense has defined the following specific objectives with regard to them:

> Iraqi compliance with all applicable U.N. Security Council Resolutions, the emergence of a government in Baghdad that respects human rights and does not threaten the peace and stability of the Gulf, and preservation of Iraq's territorial integrity. Simultaneously, the United States seeks to deter Iranian political and military adventurism; deny Iran access to sophisticated defense technologies and weaponry, particularly WMD; promote consensus among our allies and partners on the need to contain Iran; and counter Iranian-sponsored subversion and terrorism.[7]

U.S. military capabilities in the Gulf region have been substantially enhanced since 1990. There is now a larger naval presence and significant air assets are based in GCC countries. Of special note is the pre-positioning of a combat brigade set of equipment in Kuwait and the development of a similar set in Qatar. Additionally, several brigade sets of equipment are maintained afloat, available for use in either the Gulf or the Pacific region. These sets can quickly be made operational with the deployment of troops from the United States. Furthermore, the pre-positioned sets of equipment are combat ready, and forward-based naval and air presence allows for a more rapid response for emerging threats. A division base set now being established in Qatar will provide the logistical support base for the combat forces.

---

[6] U.S. Department of Defense, "U.S. Security Strategy for the Middle East" (Washington, D.C.: U.S. Department of Defense, May 1995).

[7] Ibid., p. 21.

In assessing the relevance of U.S. military deployment for addressing the Iraqi and Iranian threats, the following factors must be taken into account:

- Iranian threats in the region include: the possible interdiction of Gulf shipping (at the Strait of Hormuz), subversion of neighboring states, support for terrorism, and a potential for intimidation that would grow should Iran acquire an operational WMD capability. A coalition campaign against Iran, in case of threat to commercial shipping, would be largely maritime in character and would not require a large ground force. Given the significant American deterrence capability and the fact that Iran itself stands to lose much with the disruption of shipping in the Gulf, subversion through psychological operations, active intelligence operations, and support for terrorism would seem to be the primary policy instrument available to Iran for use against the GCC states in the near future.

- The most serious potential military threat is still an Iraqi invasion of Kuwait. The United States maintains the capability to decisively defeat Iraq, as Operation Desert Storm demonstrated, and it would likely enjoy broad international support in employing it again should Iraq attempt another invasion. Currently, the U.S. deployment is aimed primarily at reducing response time of U.S. forces, increasing U.S. capability to defend Kuwait if invasion becomes imminent, and deterring Iraq by underscoring the American commitment to the region. Here again, the U.S. air and naval forces in the region accomplish much of that task although, the pre-positioned equipment for ground forces in Kuwait and Qatar unquestionably has value as an deterrent. The United States certainly cannot tolerate the capture of a "full brigade worth" of high-tech equipment by the Iraqi army in case of a surprise invasion—and the Iraqis must know this.

- Significant, but less visible, improvements in command, control, communications, and intelligence (C_3I) capability in the Gulf has increased since (and in part due to) Operation Desert Storm. This often overlooked asset provides improved operational capability in the region.

- Since 1991, the Air Force presence in northern Saudi Arabia, which accounts for the majority of U.S. military personnel in the kingdom, has been primarily occupied with enforcing the no-fly zone in southern Iraq.

REGIONAL TRENDS FACING U.S. POLICY
IN THE PERSIAN GULF

1. The Arab Context

Despite continued divisions within the Arab world, rivalries within the GCC, and differences between the interests of GCC states and those of other Arab states, the Arab context is still important in Gulf politics. It is unlikely that the Gulf War would have contributed nearly as much to the overall U.S. goal of regional stability without the participation of Egypt, Syria, and other Arab states. Since the war, the continued involvement of Syria and Egypt in discussions on Gulf security, together with new cooperation from Jordan, has facilitated the implementation of U.S. policy and arguably has muted criticism of the American military presence in the Gulf. Cooperation with Cairo and Damascus continues, but it is a political rather than a military effort.

While public opinion in the Gulf is not identical to that in the Levant or North Africa on issues of Iraq, Iran, Israel, and economic and social reform, many international matters tend to bring the Gulf states and their Arab brethren together, especially during times of tension. The broader the Arab world's consensus about American Gulf policy, the better. Unfortunately, even the GCC consensus on U.S. Gulf policy has diminished since Desert Storm because of frustration with the Arab-Israeli peace process, humanitarian concern for the plight of the Iraqi people, and other disagreements on policies toward Iraq.

All this makes shoring up the Middle East peace process even more urgent. The "two pillar" policy of the 1970s, constructing Gulf security on the pillars of the shah's Iran and Saudi Arabia, together with some of the GCC states, was reduced to a single pillar by the

Iranian Revolution. Steps toward the construction of a new second pillar have been taken, as the 1996 deployment of U.S. Air Force aircraft to eastern Jordan suggests. But progress toward Arab-Israeli peace is essential if that pillar—which provides a vector through Jordan and Israel and to Iraq—is to be strengthened.

2. Specific Threats

American military presence and planning deter threats of invasion by Iraq and Iran against the GCC states. But these small states cannot defend themselves against either potential aggressor without U.S. assistance. Moreover, they cannot try to balance Iraq's power with that of Iran—a state at odds with its GCC neighbors on many important issues. Threats to the GCC states by Iraq and Iran, of the sort that cause short-term fluctuations in the oil market, are likely to continue.

In the case of Iraq, international sanctions have taken their toll—especially on its people—and have made recovery from the Gulf war more difficult. The Kurds in the north and the Shi'ites in the south have paid the heaviest price. The vacuum of power created in the north, and the continued conflict between the two main Kurdish groups, the Patriotic Union of Kurdistan (PUK) and the Kurdistan Democratic Party (KDP), have helped both Iran and the Turkish Kurdistan Workers Party (PKK) to make inroads in this area. The Iraqi government's intervention on the KDP's behalf in the city of Irbil in August 1996, the PUK's solicitation of Iranian help, and Turkey's move to establish a "security zone" in northern Iraq highlighted the volatility of the status quo in the region.

Analysts have tracked a gradual disintegration of Iraqi society. There has been an outflow of up to three million people, mostly educated professionals. Iraq's GDP dropped from about $60 billion in 1989 to $18 billion in 1995. The official value of the Iraqi currency, the dinar, was $3.20 before the Gulf War. It has since traded for as little as 3,000 to the dollar, but fluctuates around 1,000 to the dollar. In spite of this, Iraq has repaired much of its infrastructure, especially agriculture and light industry. If sanctions ease, Iraq could easily return to prewar oil production of three million barrels per day within two years.

The most serious burden the country faces is financial. Iraq is burdened with heavy international debts—it owes $80 billion to European countries alone. In addition, claims from Kuwait total $200 billion and there are Iranian demands for $900 billion in compensation for the Iran-Iraq war, although full repayment of either claim is highly unlikely. In any event, even with oil production fully restarted, Iraq's economic recovery will be painstaking.

Militarily, international sanctions and implementation of U.N. resolutions reportedly have destroyed most of Iraq's WMD program, although some experts worry that Iraq is covertly continuing some aspects of its nonconventional weapons program. Recent reports by UNSCOM indicate continuation of an Iraqi pattern of attempting to deceive the United Nations about its WMD programs. Iraq's conventional capabilities have been substantially weakened because of the unavailability of spare parts and losses incurred during the Gulf war, but Iraqi forces have been reorganized and remain capable of defeating GCC neighbors—in the first instance, Kuwait—in the absence of American participation.

Despite an apparent upsurge in tribal and clan politics in Iraq, the regime of Saddam Hussein remains in charge. Some argue that Saddam's rule has recently been strengthened by his successful thwarting of a series of attempted ousters orchestrated from the outside. They assert that the United States must recognize that the only people capable of bringing about the fall of the top leadership are members of the ruling elite in Saddam's power base, which includes the Ba'ath party, the intelligence community, and the military.

As for Iran, which is only beginning to recover economically from the chaos of the revolution and the devastation of the eight-year Iran-Iraq war, it is also experiencing economic hardship. Much of the hardship results from the regime's economic mismanagement and corruption, and some from international sanctions—although international cooperation with the United States on the sanctions has been limited. Iran's economic growth rate is reported to have averaged 2.7 percent over the last several years, but there has actually been a decline in per capita income because of rapid population growth. The country has been meeting its repayment schedules for foreign debt, and this has cut into its military spending. Yet, the United States maintains that Iran has increased its sponsorship of terrorism, and its drive to acquire weapons of mass destruction and the missiles that deliver them.

Stated U.S. policy toward Iran does not call for the removal of its Islamic government, although Washington still hopes for a more moderate regime. Washington did not view Iran's readiness in 1995 for a large oil development deal with an American oil company, its role in persuading the Lebanese Hizbullah militants to enter into a cease-fire with Israel in May 1996, or its apparent role in a deal with Israel on exchanging bodies of those killed on the fighting in southern Lebanon that July as signals warranting positive responses. On the contrary, Washington's own signals, including congressional allocations and publicly debated support for covert operations in Iran and the Iran and Libya Sanctions Act, have led many in Iran to believe that the overthrow of the government in Tehran remains an American objective.

Declared U.S. objectives for Iran include: discouraging it from sponsoring terrorism and subversion, preventing it from acquiring WMD, and ending its opposition to the Arab-Israeli peace process. In pursuit of these, the United States has gradually strengthened its economic sanctions against Iran. American strategy appears to operate on two basic premises: that there are no moderates in the Iranian government, and that depriving Iran of financial resources limits its ability to sponsor terrorism and seek weapons of mass destruction.

The United States is at odds with many of its allies over sanctions. This tension provides opportunities for others, such as China and Russia, to expand relations with Iran. U.S. incentives to alter Iranian behavior could produce dividends; the question is whether the time has yet arrived. Toughness alone is not likely to curb either terrorism or the pursuit of WMD, and U.S. isolation regarding many of its policies—combined with Iran's lackluster domestic situation—suggest that the time may be ripe for the United States to reconsider its current policy. However, existing sanctions and congressional views may constrain its ability to do so.

Some have expressed concern that Iran and Iraq, under pressure from the United States, might find common cause in ways that could be even more damaging to the Arab-Israeli peace process and Gulf security. This is unlikely. Deep mutual animosity remains. While there may be tactical alignments of policy, Baghdad and Tehran are unlikely to forge a lasting strategic cooperation.

3. Internal Security in the GCC States

Most outsiders believe that the GCC states face a challenging future. There is little chance that these states will develop economies not based on oil, and they currently depend on oil and gas for more than two-thirds of their government revenues. Their populations are growing rapidly, and productivity and wages are flat or declining. Real oil prices are unlikely to rise substantially over the next decade. Yet, GCC states continue to spend 15 to 30 percent of state revenues on defense.

High public-sector employment has long been a tradition in the Gulf states. In Kuwait, for example, 80 percent of the indigenous work force is employed by the state. In Saudi Arabia, the figure is over 50 percent. The rapid growth of the indigenous labor force in GCC states—among the highest in the world—will continue to strain governments' capabilities and could lead to serious unemployment, particularly if the nationals persist in scorning jobs customarily filled by foreign workers.

Oil wealth has also skewed wages, further inhibiting the development of the labor market and the economy in general. The GCC states cannot control world oil prices, and outside the oil sector, Gulf states lack areas of comparative advantage that could jump-start the private sector. All these problems are compounded by the increasing scarcity of water available to burgeoning populations. Recently it has been said that more than $100 billion dollars could be spent over the next 15 years in the Gulf building new power and water plants to meet the demands of the growing population.[8]

---

[8] U.A.E. Minister of Water and Electricity Humaid bin Naser al-Owais, Dubai, January 1996. Desalination contributes more than half of the region's domestic and industrial water, but many existing desalination plants need upgrading. In 1990 it was estimated that $30 billion was required to build desalination plants and that over $20 billion will be required after the year 2000 to replace the many aging plants built between 1975–85. See Jamil Al-Alawi and Mohammed Abdulrazzak, "Water in the Arabian Peninsula: Problems and Perspectives," in Peter Rogers and Peter Lydon (eds.), *Water in the Arab*

The Middle East as a whole has been unsuccessful in attracting foreign investment.[9] The Gulf region has attracted more than the rest of the Middle East but still not enough. Complicating matters is the fact that much of the private capital held by citizens in the region is invested outside the region, at a time when new investments—across the board, including in the oil industry—are essential.

Since the mid 1980s, the relative decline of state revenues in some GCC countries has caused the distribution of resources to shift. Resources that accrue directly to the state, such as oil earnings, have declined relative to sources of revenue that accrue to private individuals. In the early 1980s, Saudi Arabia held well over $100 billion in foreign reserves and issued no government bonds. Today foreign reserves are around $70 billion and the government has accumulated nearly $100 billion in domestic debt.

In the past, GCC governments provided generous services and material rewards to their populations, but offered relatively little in the way of political participation. Faced with declining benefits from rulers and depressing economic forecasts, popular demands for political participation will likely increase. These pressures will elicit some sort of state response, which could range from an attempt to maintain the status quo to the granting of broader participation in decision making to moves to repress challengers of the regime. Each of these possibilities could be destabilizing.

4. Political Challenges Within the GCC States

The absence of legitimate vehicles for opposition has channeled opposition forces underground or into the mosques in many Middle Eastern countries. In the GCC as a whole, there have generally been four interest groups that interact with the ruling families: merchant families, the religious establishment, the tribes, and liberal technocrats. The oil boom brought merchants great wealth in exchange for

World: Perspectives and Prognoses (Cambridge, Mass.: Division of Applied Sciences, Harvard University 1994), pp. 191–92.

[9] The entire Middle East attracts less than 3 percent of all foreign investment in the developing world, comparable to Africa's share. This contrasts with 10 percent for Eastern Europe and Central Asia, 26 percent for Latin America and the Caribbean, and 58 percent for East and South Asia. See World Bank, *Claiming Our Future: Choosing Prosperity for the Middle East and North Africa* (Washington, D.C.: World Bank, 1995), p. 7.

continued loyalty to the ruler. As oil came to dominate the Gulf economies, the economic fortunes of the merchants depended heavily on the state. While today, particularly in Kuwait and Saudi Arabia, merchants rely less on government spending for their revenues, the government increasingly needs them to invest more in their country, but such opportunities have not been as lucrative as abroad. The merchants could, therefore, become a powerful and important group in this post–oil boom period, especially as the members of the ruling family and the merchant class vie for business opportunities that are so vital to the economy's expansion.

In most GCC states, the Islamic groups can be divided into three categories: establishment Islam, which supports the status quo; reformers, including some technocrats, who invoke Islam to fight corruption and urge a redistribution of wealth; and militants, who are hostile to the ruling families and seek their demise. These three categories should not be seen as completely distinct. Islamist militants emerge from "establishment Islam" educational institutions and frequently find employment in the states' extensive religious bureaucracies. All the GCC states have recently taken steps to reassert government control over these institutions as a way to monitor and control Islamist political dissent. The amount of public support the militants garner will depend in some measure on how positively the government responds to the demands of the reformers.

The other two groups, the tribes and liberal technocrats, are not nearly so influential or independent as the merchants and Islamic groups (although both of those are also tied to the ruling regimes in important ways). The GCC rulers have succeeded in maintaining an ideology of "tribalism" while gutting the independent power of the actual tribes. Tribalism remains a strong element of social identity in all these countries, but it has lost its previous, pre-oil power to serve as an independent political force capable of mobilizing people for or against the state. The governments have settled the tribes—there is scarcely any nomadism on the Arabian Peninsula today—and thus have more control over them. Tribal leaders have become de facto state employees, enjoying the patronage of the rulers but dependent on them for political influence and the material benefits that they then pass on to their tribesmen. The states can also bypass the tribal leaders, dealing directly with individual tribesmen by giving them jobs and material benefits. Tribalism is no threat to the stability of the GCC regimes.

The political clout of liberal technocrats is completely tied to the ruling regimes, which place them in their positions of influence and can choose whether or not to listen to their advice. While they are an influential group in Gulf policy debates, they hardly have the cohesion or organizational structures to act as a bloc in the domestic politics of the Gulf states. Only in Kuwait are they afforded the opportunity to organize and contest for parliamentary seats (the "Democratic Forum" group). As of now, while they include critics of corruption and mismanagement in the ruling circles, they generally see their interests as much closer to the rulers' than to the most serious challengers for political power, the Islamist movements. Therefore, liberal technocrats can generally be counted on to support the political status quo. In the future, this social group might become more vocal in its demands for better participatory institutions, but as of now its political input is more on an individual than an organized group basis.

Many in the GCC states understand the need for American forces in the Gulf and see common interests with the United States on some regional security issues. However, suspicions of American intentions are strong, and public opinion opposes U.S. foreign policy on a range of political matters such as Bosnia, Chechnya, and the future of the Palestinian people, as well as cultural and religious matters. These contentious issues give opposition forces ammunition in their campaign to discredit GCC leadership. Thereby they create additional challenges for the American presence in the region. In sum, the greater the number of issues of contention, the larger the internal threat to the U.S. presence will be.

THE INTERNATIONAL CHALLENGES FACING U.S. POLICY IN THE GULF

It is a mistake to conclude that with the demise of the Soviet Union, the United States will be the only important outside player in the region.

1. Asia is consuming a rising amount of Middle East oil, and this trend could affect the political and military strategies available to all Gulf countries and their consumers. Unable to compete with the United States in conventional military and security guarantees, the nature of the relationship between Asia and the Gulf will develop differently than the present Western-Gulf alliance. For example, many Asian countries (primarily China) are not as sensitive to Western concerns regarding Iran and Iraq and are, therefore, more likely to provide them with economic and military assistance. China's long-term oil needs and Iran's drive to acquire missiles and weapons of mass destruction might bring these states closer together. That said, an Asian collision with U.S. interests in the Gulf is not inevitable. It is logical to assume that as China's oil imports grow, China's interest in a stable global oil market and a stable Gulf region will grow along with it.

2. India, Pakistan, Russia, and Central Asian countries are becoming more active in trade and investment in the Gulf region. This may eventually bring about new regional coalitions. The construction of an important railway between Iran and Central Asia in 1996 may significantly increase economic links with Central Asia. The strategy of isolating Iraq and Iran has pushed both states toward Russia, which seeks repayment on Baghdad's substantial debt and which, despite U.S. objections, has moved to conclude financially lucrative nuclear reactor deals with Iran. Given the uncertainty about Russia's own future, these relationships could become significant problems for the United States. The role played by Russia in preventing a U.N. Security Council resolution condemning the Iraqi military operations in the Kurdish areas of northern Iraq in September 1996 is one example of the critical stances Russia may adopt in the future.

3. Nonetheless, the United States and the GCC continue to pay most of the direct costs of defending oil supplies. The United States is also the *single* largest importer of GCC oil and has the lion's share of capital investment in the regional oil industry, research and development, production of oil pipeline construction, refinery construction, operations, and marketing.

For all these reasons, it will become progressively more costly and complex for the United States to pursue what are increasingly viewed as unilateral policies in the region.

CONCLUSION

The Gulf is an integral part of the broader "New Middle East." Many links connect the Arab-Israeli peace process with "purely" Gulf issues. The security and stability of the Gulf region impacts global stability because of its vast energy reserves. The proliferation of weapons of mass destruction in the Gulf could also affect global security.

America's strategic interests in the Gulf are clear, and American forces will remain on duty in the region to support those interests for the indefinite future. This in itself guarantees friction between the United States and Iran and Iraq, the two claimants to Gulf hegemony. There may be ways to reshape our military presence, some that this report has sought to identify, which will enable Washington to continue playing its role as security guarantor just as effectively without being a target for hostile nationalist sentiment in the region.

The Gulf is a cockpit of contending ambitions and it encourages emerging challenges to the status quo. It behooves the United States, therefore, to keep its Gulf policy under careful review and be prepared to modify it as necessary. Any changes, in the implementation of America's Gulf policy, however, should be carefully weighed, and U.S. friends and allies, whose own security is directly involved, should be fully consulted.

Background Materials

U.N. SECURITY COUNCIL RESOLUTION 687 (1991)

*on identification of border demarcation between Iraq and
Kuwait, also concerns the establishment of the Special
Commission,[1] the destruction of chemical and biological
weapons, IAEA inspections of nuclear capabilities, destruction
of missiles with ranges over 150 kilometres, Iraqi debt and
statement on when prohibitions against import of commodities
and products originating in Iraq (paragraph 22) will end*

*Adopted by the Security Council at its 2981st meeting on
3 November 1991*

The Security Council,

Recalling its resolutions 660 (1990) of 2 August 1990, 661 (1990) of
6 August 1990, 662 (1990), 664 (1990) of 18 August 1990, 665 of 25
August 1990, 666 (1990) of 13 September 1990, 667 (1990) of 16 September, 669 (1990) of 24 September 1990, 670 (1990) of 25 September
1990, 674 (1990) of 29 October 1990 and 677 (1990) of 28 November 1990, 678 (1990) of 29 November 1990 and 686 (1991) of
2 March 1991,

Welcoming the restoration to Kuwait of its sovereignty, independence and territorial integrity and the return of its legitimate
Government,

Affirming the commitment of all Member States to the sovereignty,
territorial integrity and political independence of Kuwait and Iraq,
and noting the intention expressed by the Member States cooperating with Kuwait under paragraph 2 of resolution 678 (1990) to bring

---

[1] *Editor's Note:* Pursuant to U.N. Council Resolution 687, the Executive Chairman
of the Special Commission submits a report every six months to the Secretary-General
on the commission's activities. The most current report covers the period from 11 October 1996 to 11 April 1997 (see United Nations S/1997/301).

their military presence in Iraq to an end as soon as possible consistent with paragraph 8 of resolution 686 (1991),

Reaffirming the need to be assured of Iraq's peaceful intentions in the light of its unlawful invasion and occupation of Kuwait,

Taking note of the letter dated 27 February 1991 from the Deputy Prime Minister and Minister of Foreign Affairs of Iraq addressed to the President of the Security Council and of his letters of the same date addressed to the President of the Council and to the Secretary-General and those letters dated 3 March and 5 March he addressed to them, pursuant to resolution 686 (1991),

Noting that Iraq and Kuwait, as independent sovereign States, signed at Baghdad on 4 October 1963 "Agreed Minutes between the State of Kuwait and the Republic of Iraq regarding the restoration of friendly relations, recognition and related matters," thereby formally recognizing the boundary between Iraq and Kuwait and the allocation of islands, which Agreed Minutes were registered with the United Nations in accordance with article 102 of the Charter of the United Nations and in which Iraq recognized the independence and complete sovereignty of the State of Kuwait which its boundaries and specified in the letter of the Prime Minister of Iraq dated 21 July 1932 and as accepted by the ruler of Kuwait in his letter dated 10 August 1932,

Conscious of the need for demarcation of the said boundary,

Conscious also of the statements by Iraq threatening to use weapons in violation of its obligations under the Protocol for the Prohibition of the Use in War of Asphyxiating, Poisonous or Other Gases, and of Bacteriological Methods of Warfare, signed at Geneva on 17 June 1925 and of its prior use of chemical weapons, and affirming that grave consequences would follow any further use by Iraq of such weapons,

Recalling that Iraq has subscribed to the Final Declaration adopted by all States participating in the Conference of States Parties to the 1925 Geneva Protocol and Other Interested States, held in Paris from 7 to 11 January 1989, establishing the objective of universal elimination of chemical and biological weapons,

[60]

Recalling also that Iraq has signed the Convention on the Prohibition of the Development, Production and Stockpiling of Bacteriological (Biological) and Toxin Weapons and on Their Destruction of 10 April 1972,

Noting the importance of Iraq ratifying the Convention,

Noting also the importance of all States adhering to the Convention and encouraging its forthcoming review conference to reinforce the authority, efficiency and universal scope of the Convention,

Stressing the importance of an early conclusion by the Conference on Disarmament of its work on a convention on the universal prohibition of chemical weapons and of universal adherence thereto,

Aware of the use by Iraq of ballistic missiles in unprovoked attacks and therefore of the need to take specific measures in regard to such missiles located in Iraq,

Concerned by the reports in the hands of Member states that Iraq has attempted to acquire materials for a nuclear-weapons programme contrary to its obligations under the Treaty on the Non-Proliferation of Nuclear Weapons of 1 July 1968,

Recalling the objective of the establishment of a nuclear weapon-free zone in the region of the Middle East,

Conscious of the threat that all weapons of mass destruction pose to peace and security in the area of the need to work toward the establishment in the Middle East of a zone free of such weapons,

Conscious also of the objective of achieving a balanced and comprehensive control of armaments in the region,

Conscious further of the importance of achieving the objectives noted above using all available means, including dialogue among the States of the region,

Noting that resolution 686 (1991) marked the lifting of measures imposed by resolution 661 (1991), many Kuwaiti and third-State nationals are still not accounted for and property remains unreturned,

Recalling the International Convention against the Taking of Hostages, opened for signature in New York on 18 December 1979, which categorizes all acts of taking hostages as manifestations of international terrorism,

Deploring threats made by Iraq during the recent conflict to make use of terrorism against targets outside Iraq and the taking of hostages by Iraq,

Taking note with grave concern of the reports transmitted by the Security-General on 20 March and 28 March 1991, and conscious of the necessity to meet urgently the humanitarian needs in Kuwait and Iraq,

Bearing in mind its objective of restoring international peace and security in the area as set out in its recent resolutions,

Conscious of the need to take the following measures acting under Chapter VII of the Charter of the Untied Nations,

A

1. *Affirms* all thirteen resolutions noted above, except as expressly changed below to achieve the goals of the present resolution, including a formal cease-fire;

2. *Demands* that Iraq and Kuwait respect the inviolability of the international boundary and the allocation of islands set out in the "Agreed Minutes between the State of Kuwait and the Republic of Iraq regarding the restoration of friendly relations, recognition and related matters," signed by them in the exercise of their sovereignty at Baghdad on 4 October 1963 and registered with the United Nations;

3. *Calls upon* the Secretary-General to lend his assistance to make arrangements with Iraq and Kuwait to demarcate the boundary between Iraq and Kuwait, drawing on appropriate material including the maps transmitted with the letter dated 28 March 1991 addressed to him by the Permanent Representative of the United Kingdom of Great Britain and Northern Ireland to the

United Nations; and to report back to the Council within one month;

4. *Decides* to guarantee the inviolability of the above-mentioned international boundary and to take, as appropriate, all necessary measures to that end in accordance with the Charter of the United Nations;

B

5. *Requests* the Secretary-General, after consulting with Iraq and Kuwait, to submit within three days to the Council for its approval a plan for the immediate deployment of a United Nations observer unit to monitor the Khawr'Abd Allah and a demilitarized zone, which is hereby established, extending ten kilometres into Iraq and five kilometres into Kuwait from the boundary referred to in the "Agreed Minutes between the State of Kuwait and the Republic of Iraq regarding the restoration of friendly relations, recognition and related matters"; to deter violations of the boundary through its presence in and surveillance of the demilitarized zone and to observe any hostile or potentially hostile action mounted from the territory of one State against the other; and also requests the Secretary-General to report regularly to the Council on the operations of the unit and to do so immediately if there are serious violations of the zone or potential threats to peace;

6. *Notes* that as soon as the Secretary-General notifies the Council of the completion of the deployment of the United Nations observer unit, the conditions will be established for the Member States cooperating with Kuwait in accordance with resolution 678 (1990) to bring their military presence in Iraq to an end consistent with resolution 686 (1991).

C

7. *Invites* Iraq to reaffirm unconditionally its obligations under the Protocol for the Prohibition of the Use in War of Asphyxiating, Poisonous or Other Gases, and of Bacteriological Methods of Warfare, signed at Geneva on 17 June 1925, and to ratify the Con-

vention on the Prohibition of the Development, Production and Stockpiling of Bacteriological (Biological) and Toxin Weapons and on Their Destruction, of 10 April 1972;

8. *Decides* that Iraq shall unconditionally accept the destruction, removal, or rendering harmless, under international supervision of:

   (a) All chemical and biological weapons and all stocks of agents and all related subsystems and components and all research, development, support and manufacturing facilities related thereto;

   (b) All ballistic missiles with a range greater than one hundred and fifty kilometres and related major parts and repair and production facilities

9. *Decides also,* for the implementation of paragraph 8, the following:

   (a) Iraq shall submit to the Secretary-General, within fifteen days of the adoption of the present resolution, a declaration on the locations, amounts and types of all times specified in paragraph 8 and agree to urgent, on-site inspection as specified below;

   (b) The Secretary-General, in consultation with the appropriate Governments and where appropriate, with the Director General of the World Health Organization, within forty-five days of the adoption of the present resolution shall develop and submit to the Council for approval a plan calling for the completion of the following acts within forty-five days of such approval:

      (i) The forming of a special commission which shall carry out immediate on-site inspection of Iraq's biological, chemical and missile capabilities based on Iraq's declarations and the designation of any additional locations by the special commission itself;

      (ii) The yielding by Iraq of possession to the Special Commission for destruction, removal or rendering harmless, taking into account the requirements of public safety, of all times specified under paragraph 8 (a), including items at the additional locations designated by the Special Commission under paragraph (1) and the destruction by Iraq, under the supervision of the Special Commission, of all its missile capabilities including launchers, as specified under paragraph 8 (b);

(iii) The provision by the Special Commission to the Director General of the International Atomic Energy Agency of the assistance and cooperation required in paragraphs 12 and 13;

10. *Decides further* that Iraq shall unconditionally undertake not to use, develop, construct or acquire any of the items specified in paragraphs 8 and 9, and requests the Secretary-General in consultation with the Special Commission, to develop a plan for the future ongoing monitoring and verification of Iraq's compliance with the present paragraph, to be submitted to the Council for approval within one hundred and twenty days of the passage of the present resolution.

11. *Invites* Iraq to reaffirm unconditionally its obligations under the Treaty on the Non-Proliferation of Nuclear Weapons of 1 July 1968;

12. *Decides* that Iraq shall unconditionally agree not to acquire or develop nuclear weapons or nuclear-weapon–usable material or any subsystems or components or any research, development, support or manufacturing facilities related to the above; to submit to the Secretary-General of the International Atomic Energy Agency within fifteen days of the adoption of the present resolution a declaration of the locations, amounts and types of all times specified above; to place all of its nuclear-weapon–usable materials under the exclusive control, for custody and removal, of the Agency, with the assistance and cooperation of the Special Commission as provided for in the plan of the Secretary-General discussed in paragraph 9 (b); to accept in accordance with the arrangements provided for in paragraph 13, urgent on-site

inspection and the destruction, removal or rendering harmless as appropriate of all times specified above; and to accept the plan discussed in paragraph 13 for the future ongoing monitoring and verification of its compliance with these undertakings;

13. *Requests* the Director General of the International Atomic Energy Agency, through the Secretary-General and with the assistance and cooperation of the Special Commission as provided for in the plan of the Secretary-General referred to in paragraph 9 (b), to carry out immediate on-site inspection of Iraq's nuclear capabilities based on Iraq's declaration and the designation of any additional locations by the Special Commission; to develop a plan for submission to the council within forty-five days calling for the destruction, removal or rendering harmless as appropriate of all times listed in paragraph 12; to carry out the plan within forty-five days following approval by the Council and to develop a plan, taking into account, the rights and obligations of Iraq under the treaty on the Non-Proliferation of Nuclear Weapons, for the future ongoing monitoring and verification of Iraq's compliance with paragraph 12, including an inventory of all nuclear material in Iraq subject to the Agency's verification and inspection to confirm that Agency safeguards cover all relevant nuclear activities in Iraq to be submitted to the Council for approval within one hundred and twenty days of the adoption of the present resolution;

14. *Notes* that the actions to be taken by Iraq in paragraphs 8 to 13 represent steps towards the goal of establishing in the Middle East a zone free from weapons of mass destruction and all missiles for their delivery and the objective of a global ban on chemical weapons;

D

15. *Requests* the Secretary-General to report to the Council on the steps taken to facilitate the return of all Kuwaiti property seized by Iraq, including a list of any property that Kuwait claims has not been returned or which has not been returned intact;

16. *Reaffirms* that Iraq, without prejudice to its debts and obligations arising prior to 2 August 1990, which will be addressed through the normal mechanisms, is liable under international law for any direct loss, damage—including environmental damage and the depletions of natural resources—or injury to foreign Governments, nationals and corporations as a result of its unlawful invasion and occupation of Kuwait;

17. *Decides* that all Iraq statements made since 2 August 1990 repudiating its foreign debt are null and void, and demands that Iraq adhere scrupulously to all of its obligations concerning servicing and repayment of its foreign debt;

18. *Decides also* to create a fund to pay compensation for claims that fall within paragraph 16 and to establish a commission that will administer the fund;

19. *Directs* the Secretary-General to develop and present to the Council for decision, no later than thirty days following the adoption of the present resolution, recommendations for the Fund to be established in accordance with paragraph 18 and for a programme to implement the decisions in paragraph 16 to 18, including the following: administration of the Fund; mechanisms for determining the appropriate level of Iraq's contribution to the Fund, based on a percentage of the value of its exports of petroleum and petroleum products, not to exceed a figure to be suggested to the Council by the Secretary-General, taking into account the requirement of the people of Iraq, Iraq's payment capacity as assessed in conjunction with the international financial institutions taking into consideration external debt service, and the needs of the Iraqi economy; arrangements for ensuring that payments are made to the Fund; the process by which funds will be allocated and claims paid; appropriate procedures for evaluating losses, listing claims and verifying their validity, and resolving disputed claims in respect of Iraq's liability as specified in paragraph 16; and the composition of the Commission designated above;

F

20. *Decides,* effective immediately, that the prohibitions against the sale or supply to Iraq of commodities or products other than medicine and health supplies, and prohibitions against financial transactions related thereto contained in resolution 661 (1990), shall not apply to foodstuffs notified to the Security Council Committee established by resolution 661 (1990) concerning the situation between Iraq and Kuwait or, with the approval of the that Committee, under the simplified and accelerated "no-objection" procedure, to materials and supplies for essential civilian needs as identified in the report to the Secretary-General dated 20 March 1991, and in any further findings of humanitarian need by the Committee;

21. *Decides* to review the provisions of paragraph 20 every sixty days in the light of the policies and practices of the Government of Iraq, including the implementation of all relevant resolutions of the Council, for the purpose of determining whether to reduce or lift the prohibitions referred to therein;

22. *Decides also* that upon the approval by the Council of the programme called for in paragraph 19 and upon Council agreement that Iraq has completed all actions contemplated in paragraphs 8 to 13, the prohibitions against the import of commodities and products originating in Iraq and the prohibitions against financial transactions related thereto contained in resolution 661 (1990) shall have no further force or effect;

23. *Decides further* that, pending action by the Council under paragraph 22, the Security Council Committee established by resolution 661 (1990) concerning the situation between Iraq and Kuwait shall be empowered to approve, when required to assure adequate financial resources on the part of Iraq to carry out the activities under paragraph 20, exceptions to the prohibition against the import of commodities and products originating in Iraq;

24. *Decides* that, in accordance with resolution 661 (1990) and subsequent related resolutions and until it takes a further decision,

all States shall continue to prevent the sale or supply or Iraq, or the promotion or facilitation of such sale or supply, by their nations or from their territories or using their flag vessels or aircraft, of:

(a) Arms and related *matériel* of all types, specifically including the sale or transfer through other means of all forms of conventional military equipment, including for paramilitary forces, and spare parts and components and their means of production for such equipment;

(b) Items specified and defined paragraphs 8 and 12 not otherwise covered above;

(c) Technology under licensing or other transfer arrangements used in the production, utilization or stockpiling of items specified in paragraphs 9 (a) and (b);

(d) Personnel or materials for training or technical support services relating to the design, development, manufacture, use, maintenance or support of items specified in paragraphs (a) and (b);

25. *Calls upon* all States and international organizations to act strictly in accordance with paragraph 24, notwithstanding the existence of any contracts, agreements, licenses or any other arrangements;

26. *Requests* the Secretary-General, in consultation with appropriate Governments, to develop within sixty days, for the approval of the Council, guidelines to facilitate full international implementation of paragraphs 24, 25 and 27, and to make them available to all States and to establish a procedure for updating these guidelines periodically;

27. *Calls upon* all States to maintain such national controls and procedures and to take such other actions consistent with the guidelines to be established by the Council under paragraph 26 as may be necessary to ensure compliance with the terms of paragraph 24, and calls upon international organizations to take all appropriate steps to assist in ensuring such full compliance;

28. *Agrees* to review its decisions in paragraphs 22 to 25, except for the items specified and defined in paragraphs 8 and 12, on a regular basis and in any case one hundred and twenty days following the adoption of the present resolution, taking into account Iraq's compliance with the resolution and general progress towards the control of armaments in the region;

29. *Decides* that all States, including Iraq, shall take the necessary measures to ensure that no claim shall lie at the instance of the Government of Iraq, or of any person or body in Iraq, or of any person claiming through or for the benefit of any such person or body, in connection with any contract or other transaction where its performance was affected by reason of the measures taken by the Council in resolution 661 (1990) and related resolutions;

G

30. *Decides* that, in furtherance of its commitment to facilitate the repatriation of all Kuwaiti and third-State nationals, Iraq shall extend all necessary cooperation to the International Committee of the Red Cross by providing lists of such persons, facilitating the access of the International Committee to all such persons wherever located or detained and facilitating the search by the International Committee for those Kuwaiti and third-State national still unaccounted for;

31. *Invites* the International Committee of the Red Cross to keep the Secretary-General apprised, as appropriate, of all activities undertaken in connection with facilitating the repatriation or return of all Kuwaiti and third-State nationals or their remains present in Iraq on or after 2 August 1990;

32. *Requires* Iraq to inform the council that it will not commit or support any act of international terrorism or allow any organization directed towards commission of such acts to operate within its territory and to condemn unequivocally and renounce all acts, methods and practices of terrorism;

33. *Declares* that, upon official notification by Iraq to the Secretary-General and to the Security Council of its acceptance of the above provisions, a formal cease-fire is effective between Iraq and Kuwait and the Member States cooperating with Kuwait in accordance with resolution 678 (1990);

34. *Decides* to remain seized of the matter and to take such further steps as may be required for the implementation of the present resolution and to secure peace and security in the region.

U.N. SECURITY COUNCIL RESOLUTION 986 (1995)

on authorization to permit the import of petroleum and petroleum products originating in Iraq, as a temporary measure to provide for humanitarian needs of the Iraqi people

Adopted by the Security Council at its 3519th meeting on 14 April 1995

The Security Council,

Recalling its previous relevant resolutions,

Concerned by the serious nutritional and health situation of the Iraqi population, and by the risk of a further deterioration in this situation,

Convinced of the need as a temporary measure to provide for the humanitarian needs of the Iraqi people until the fulfillment by Iraq of the relevant Security Council resolutions, including notably resolution 687 (1991) of 3 April 1991, allows the Council to take further action with regard to the prohibitions referred to in resolution 661 (1990) of 6 August 1990, in accordance with the provisions of those resolutions,

Convinced also of the need for equitable distribution of humanitarian relief to all segments of the Iraqi population throughout the country,

Reaffirming the commitment of all Member States to the sovereignty and territorial integrity of Iraq,

Acting under Chapter VII of the Charter of the United Nations,

1. *Authorizes* States, notwithstanding the provisions of paragraphs 3 (a), 3 (b) and 4 of resolution 661 (1990) and subsequent relevant resolutions, to permit the import of petroleum and petro-

leum products originating in Iraq, including financial and other essential transactions directly relating thereto, sufficient to produce a sum not exceeding a total of one billion United States dollars every 90 days for the purposes set out in this resolution and subject to the following conditions:

(a) Approval by the Committee established by resolution 661 (1990), in order to ensure the transparency of each transaction and its conformity with the other provisions of this resolution, after submission of an application by the State concerned, endorsed by the Government of Iraq, for each proposed purchase of Iraqi petroleum and petroleum products, including details of the purchase price at fair market value, the export route, the opening of a letter of credit payable to the escrow account to be established by the Secretary-General for the purposes of this resolution, and of any other directly related financial or other essential transaction;

(b) Payment of the full amount of each purchase of Iraqi petroleum and petroleum products directly by the purchaser in the State concerned into the escrow account to be established by the Secretary-General for the purposes of this resolution;

2. *Authorizes* Turkey, notwithstanding the provisions of paragraphs 3 (a), 3 (b) and 4 of resolution 661 (1990) and the provisions of paragraph 1 above, to permit the import of petroleum and petroleum products originating in Iraq sufficient, after the deduction of the percentage referred to in paragraph 8 (c) below for the Compensation Fund, to meet the pipeline tariff charges, verified as reasonable by the independent inspection agents referred to in paragraph 6 below, for the transport of Iraqi petroleum and petroleum products through the Kirkuk-Yumurtalik pipeline in Turkey authorized by paragraph 1 above;

3. *Decides* that paragraphs 1 and 2 of this resolution shall come into force at 00.01 Eastern Standard Time on the day after the President of the Council has informed the members of the Council that he has received the report from the Secretary-General requested in paragraph 13 below, and shall remain in force

for an initial period of 180 days unless the Council takes other relevant action with regard to the provisions of resolution 661 (1990);

4. *Further decides* to conduct a thorough review of all aspects of the implementation of this resolution 90 days after the entry into force of paragraph 1 above and again prior to the end of the initial 180 day period, on receipt of the reports referred to in paragraphs 11 and 12 below, and expresses its intention, prior to the end of the 180 day period, to consider favourably renewal of the provisions of this resolution, provided that the reports referred to in paragraphs 11 and 12 below indicate that those provisions are being satisfactorily implemented;

5. *Further decides* that the remaining paragraphs of this resolution shall come into force forthwith;

6. *Directs* the Committee established by resolution 661 (1990) to monitor the sale of petroleum and petroleum products to be exported by Iraq via the Kirkuk-Yumurtalik pipeline from Iraq to Turkey and from the Mina al-Bakr oil terminal, with the assistance of independent inspection agents appointed by the Secretary-General, who will keep the Committee informed of the amount of petroleum and petroleum products exported from Iraq after the date of entry into force of paragraph 1 of this resolution, and will verify that the purchase price of the petroleum and petroleum products is reasonable in the light of prevailing market conditions, and that, for the purposes of the arrangements set out in this resolution, the larger share of the petroleum and petroleum products is shipped via the Kirkuk-Yumurtalik pipeline and the remainder is exported from the Mina al-Bakr oil terminal;

7. *Requests* the Secretary-General to establish an escrow account for the purposes of this resolution, to appoint independent and certified public accountants to audit it, and to keep the Government of Iraq fully informed;

8. *Decides* that the funds in the escrow account shall be used to meet the humanitarian needs of the Iraqi population and for the fol-

lowing other purposes, and requests the Secretary-General to use the funds deposited in the escrow account:

(a) To finance the export to Iraq, in accordance with the procedures of the Committee established by resolution 661 (1990), of medicine, health supplies, foodstuffs, and materials and supplies for essential civilian needs, as referred to in paragraph 20 of resolution 687 (1991) provided that:

    (i) Each export of goods is at the request of the Government of Iraq;

    (ii) Iraq effectively guarantees their equitable distribution, on the basis of a plan submitted to and approved by the Secretary-General, including a description of the goods to be purchased;

    (iii) The Secretary-General receives authenticated confirmation that the exported goods concerned have arrived in Iraq;

(b) To complement, in view of the exceptional circumstances prevailing in the three Governorates mentioned below, the distribution by the Government of Iraq of goods imported under this resolution, in order to ensure an equitable distribution of humanitarian relief to all segments of the Iraqi population throughout the country, by providing between 130 million and 150 million United States dollars every 90 days to the United Nations Inter-Agency Humanitarian Programme operating within the sovereign territory of Iraq in the three northern Governorates of Dihouk, Arbil and Suleimaniyeh, except that if less than one billion United States dollars worth of petroleum or petroleum products is sold during any 90 day period, the Secretary-General may provide a proportionately smaller amount for this purpose;

(c) To transfer to the Compensation Fund the same percentage of the funds deposited in the escrow account as that decided by the Council in paragraph 2 of resolution 705 (1991) of 15 August 1991;

(d) To meet the costs to the United Nations of the independent inspection agents and the certified public accountants and the activities associated with implementation of this resolution;

(e) To meet the current operating costs of the Special Commission, pending subsequent payment in full of the costs of carrying out the tasks authorized by section C of resolution 687 (1991);

(f) To meet any reasonable expenses, other than expenses payable in Iraq, which are determined by the Committee established by resolution 661 (1990) to be directly related to the export by Iraq of petroleum and petroleum products permitted under paragraph 1 above or to the export to Iraq, and activities directly necessary therefor, of the parts and equipment permitted under paragraph 9 below;

(g) To make available up to 10 million United States dollars every 90 days from the funds deposited in the escrow account for the payments envisaged under paragraph 6 of resolution 778 (1992) of 2 October 1992;

9. *Authorizes* States to permit, notwithstanding the provisions of paragraph 3 (c) of resolution 661 (1990):

(a) The export to Iraq of the parts and equipment which are essential for the safe operation of the Kirkuk-Yumurtalik pipeline system in Iraq, subject to the prior approval by the Committee established by resolution 661 (1990) of each export contract;

(b) Activities directly necessary for the exports authorized under subparagraph (a) above, including financial transactions related thereto;

10. *Decides* that, since the costs of the exports and activities authorized under paragraph 9 above are precluded by paragraph 4 of resolution 661 (1990) and by paragraph 11 of resolution 778 (1991) from being met from funds frozen in accordance with those provisions, the cost of such exports and account established for the purposes of this resolution, and following approval in each case

by the Committee established by resolution 661 (1990), exceptionally be financed by letters of credit, drawn against future oil sales the proceeds of which are to be deposited in the escrow account;

11. *Requests* the Secretary-General to report to the Council 90 days after the date of entry into force of paragraph 1 above, and again prior to the end of the initial 180 day period, on the basis of observation by United Nations personnel in Iraq, and on the basis of consultations with the Government of Iraq, on whether Iraq has ensured the equitable distribution of medicine, health supplies, foodstuffs, and materials and supplies for essential civilian needs, financed in accordance with paragraph 8 (a) above, including in his reports any observations he may have on the adequacy of the revenues to meet Iraq's humanitarian needs, and on Iraq's capacity to export sufficient quantities of petroleum and petroleum products to produce the sum referred to in paragraph 1 above;

12. *Requests* the Committee established by resolution 661 (1990), in close coordination with the Secretary-General, to develop expedited procedures as necessary to implement the arrangements in paragraphs 1, 2, 6, 8, 9 and 10 of this resolution and to report to the Council 90 days after the date of entry into force of paragraph 1 above and again prior to the end of the initial 180 day period on the implementation of those arrangements;

13. *Requests* the Secretary-General to take the actions necessary to ensure the effective implementation of this resolution, authorizes him to enter into any necessary arrangements or agreements, and requests him to report to the Council when he has done so;

14. *Decides* that petroleum and petroleum products subject to this resolution shall while under Iraqi title be immune from legal proceedings and not be subject to any form of attachment, garnishment or execution, and that all States shall take any steps that may be necessary under their respective domestic legal systems to assure this protection, and to ensure that the proceeds of the sale are not diverted from the purposes laid down in this resolution;

15. *Affirms* that the escrow account established for the purposes of this resolution enjoys the privileges and immunities of the United Nations;

16. *Affirms* that all persons appointed by the Secretary-General for the purpose of implementing this resolution enjoy privileges and immunities as experts on mission for the United Nations in accordance with the Convention on the Privileges and Immunities of the United Nations, and requires the Government of Iraq to allow them full freedom of movement and all necessary facilities for the discharge of their duties in the implementation of this resolution;

17. *Affirms* that nothing in this resolution affects Iraq's duty scrupulously to adhere to all of its obligations concerning servicing and repayment of its foreign debt, in accordance with the appropriate international mechanisms;

18. *Also affirms* that nothing in this resolution should be construed as infringing the sovereignty or territorial integrity of Iraq;

19. *Decides* to remain seized of the matter.

U.N. SECURITY COUNCIL RESOLUTION 1051 (1996)

on approval of the mechanism for monitoring Iraqi imports and exports, pursuant to Security Council resolutions and decisions 715 (1991)

Adopted by the Security Council at its 3644th meeting on 27 March 1996

The Security Council,

Reaffirming its resolution 687 (1991) of 8 April 1991, and in particular section C thereof, its resolution 707 (1991) of 15 August 1991 and its resolution 715 (1991) of 11 October 1991 and the plans for ongoing monitoring and verification approved thereunder,

Recalling the request in paragraph 7 of its resolution 715 (1991) to the Committee established under resolution 661 (1990), the Special Commission and the Director General of the International Atomic Energy Agency (IAEA) to develop in cooperation a mechanism for monitoring any future sales or supplies by other countries to Iraq of items relevant to the implementation of section C of resolution 687 (1991) and other relevant resolutions, including resolution 715 (1991) and the plans approved thereunder,

Having considered the letter of 7 December 1995 (S/1995/1017) to the President of the Council from the Chairman of the Committee established under resolution 661 (1990), annex I of which contains the provisions for the mechanism for export/import monitoring called for in paragraph 7 of resolution 715 (1991),

Recognizing that the export/import monitoring mechanism is an integral part of ongoing monitoring and verification by the Special Commission and the IAEA,

Recognizing that the export/import mechanism is not a regime for international licensing, but rather for the timely provision of information by States in which companies are located which are contemplating sales or supplies to Iraq of items covered by the plans for ongoing monitoring and verification and will not impede Iraq's legitimate right to import or export for non-proscribed purposes, items and technology necessary for the promotion of its economic and social development,

Acting under Chapter VII of the Charter of the United Nations,

1. *Approves*, pursuant to the relevant provisions of its resolutions 687 (1991) and 715 (1991), the provisions for the monitoring mechanism contained in annex I of the aforementioned letter of 7 December 1995 (S/1995/1017), subject to the terms of this resolution;

2. *Approves* also the general principles to be followed in implementing the monitoring mechanism contained in the letter of 17 July 1995 from the Chairman of the Special Commission to the Chairman of the Committee established under resolution 661 (1990) which is contained in annex II of the aforementioned letter of 7 December 1995 (S/1995/1017);

3. *Affirms* that the mechanism approved by this resolution is without prejudice to and shall not impair the operation of existing or future non-proliferation agreements or regimes on the international or regional level including arrangements referred to in resolution 687 (1991), nor shall such agreements or regimes impair the operation of the mechanism;

4. *Confirms*, until the Council decides otherwise under its relevant resolutions, that requests by other States for sales to Iraq or requests by Iraq for import of any item or technology to which the mechanism applies shall continue to be addressed to the Committee established under resolution 661 (1990) for decision by that Committee in accordance with paragraph 4 of the mechanism;

5. *Decides*, subject to paragraphs 4 and 7 of this resolution, that all States shall:

(a) Transmit to the joint unit constituted by the Special Commission and the Director General of the IAEA under paragraph 16 of the mechanism the notifications, with the data from potential exporters, and all other relevant information when available to the States, as requested in the mechanism on the intended sale or supply from their territories of any items or technologies which are subject to such notification in accordance with paragraphs 9, 11, 13, 24, 25, 27 and 28 of the mechanism;

(b) Report to the joint unit, in accordance with paragraphs 13, 24, 25, 27 and 28 of the mechanism, any information they may have at their disposal or may receive from suppliers in their territories of attempts to circumvent the mechanism or to supply Iraq with items prohibited to Iraq under the plans for ongoing monitoring and verification approved by resolution 715 (1991), or where the procedures for special exceptions laid down in paragraphs 24 and 25 of the mechanism have not been followed by Iraq;

6. *Decides* that the notifications required under paragraph 5 above shall be provided to the joint unit by Iraq, in respect of all items and technologies referred to in paragraph 12 of the mechanism, as from the date agreed upon between the Special Commission and the Director General of the IAEA and Iraq, and in any event not later than sixty days after the adoption of this resolution;

7. *Decides* that the notifications required under paragraph 5 above shall be provided to the joint unit by all other States as from the date the Secretary-General and the Director General of the IAEA, after their consultations with the members of the Council and other interested States, report to the Council indicating that they are satisfied with the preparedness of States for the effective implementation of the mechanism;

8. *Decides* that the information provided through the mechanism shall be treated as confidential and restricted to the Special Commission and the IAEA, to the extent that this is consistent with their respective responsibilities under resolution 715 (1991),

other relevant resolutions and the plans for ongoing monitoring and verification approved under resolution 715 (1991);

9. *Affirms*, if experience over time demonstrates the need or new technologies so require, that the Council would be prepared to review the mechanism in order to determine whether any changes are required and that the annexes to the plans for ongoing monitoring and verification approved under resolution 715 (1991), which identify the items and technologies to be notified under the mechanism, may be amended in accordance with the plans, after appropriate consultations with interested States and, as laid down in the plans, after notification to the Council;

10. *Decides* also that the Committee established under resolution 661 (1990) and the Special Commission shall carry out the functions assigned to them under the mechanism, until the Council decides otherwise;

11. *Requests* the Director General of the IAEA to carry out, with the assistance and cooperation of the Special Commission, the functions assigned to him under the mechanism; calls upon all States and international organizations to cooperate fully with the Committee established under resolution 661 (1990), the Special Commission and the Director General of the IAEA in the fulfillment of their tasks in connection with the mechanism, including supplying such information as may be sought by them in implementation of the mechanism;

12. *Calls upon* all States to adopt as soon as possible such measures as may be necessary under their national procedures to implement the mechanism;

13. *Decides* that all States shall, not later than 45 days after the adoption of this resolution, be provided by the Special Commission and the Director General of the IAEA with information necessary to make preparatory arrangements at the national level prior to the implementation of the provisions of the mechanism;

14. *Demands* that Iraq meet unconditionally all its obligations under the mechanism approved by this resolution and cooper-

ate fully with the Special Commission and the Director General of the IAEA in the carrying out of their tasks under this resolution and the mechanism by such means as they may determine in accordance with their mandates from the Council;

15. *Decides* to consolidate the periodic requirements for progress reports under its resolutions 699 (1991), 715 (1991) and this resolution and to request the Secretary-General and the Director General of the IAEA to submit such consolidated progress reports every six months to the Council, commencing on 11 April 1996;

16. *Decides* to remain seized of the matter.

U.N. SECURITY COUNCIL RESOLUTION 1060 (1996)

on Iraq's refusal to allow access to sites designated by the Special Commission

Adopted by the Security Council at its 3672nd meeting on 12 June 1996.

The Security Council,

Recalling all its previous relevant resolutions, and in particular its resolutions 687 (1991) of 3 April 1991, 707 (1991) of 15 August 1991 and 715 (1991) of 11 October 1991,

Recalling also the letter from the Executive Chairman of the United Nations Special Commission to the President of the Security Council of 9 March 1996 (S/1996/182), the letter from the President of the Security Council to the Executive Chairman of the Special Commission of 12 March 1996 (S/1996/183), the statement made at its 3642nd meeting on 19 March 1996 by the President of the Security Council (S/PRST/1996/11), and the report of the Chairman of the Special Commission of 11 April 1996 (S/1996/258),

Reiterating the commitment of all Member States to the sovereignty, territorial integrity and political independence of Kuwait and Iraq,

Recalling in this context the notes from the Secretary-General of 21 July 1993 (S/26127) and 1 December 1993 (S/26825),

Noting the progress made in the work of the Special Commission towards the elimination of Iraq programmes of weapons of mass destruction, and outstanding problems, reported by the Chairman of the Special Commission,

Noting with concern the incidents on 11 and 12 June 1996, reported to members of the Council by the Executive Chairman of the

Special Commission, when access by a Special Commission inspection team to sites in Iraq designated for inspection by the Commission was excluded by the Iraqi authorities,

Emphasizing the importance the Council attaches to full compliance by Iraq with its obligations under resolutions 687 (1991), 707 (1991) and 715 (1991) to permit immediate, unconditional and unrestricted access to the Special Commission to any site which the Commission wishes to inspect,

Emphasizing the unacceptability of any attempts by Iraq to deny access to any such site,

Acting under Chapter VII of the Charter of the United Nations,

1. *Deplores* the refusal of the Iraqi authorities to allow access to sites designated by the Special Commission, which constitutes a clear violation of the provisions of Security Council resolutions 687 (1991), 707 (1991) and 715 (1991);

2. *Demands* that Iraq cooperate fully with the Special Commission in accordance with the relevant resolutions; and that the Government of Iraq allow the Special Commission inspection teams immediate, unconditional and unrestricted access to any and all areas, facilities, equipment, records and means of transportation which they wish to inspect;

3. *Expresses* its full support to the Special Commission in its efforts to ensure implementation of its mandate under the relevant resolutions of the Council;

4. *Decides* to remain seized of the matter.

ANTHONY LAKE,
"CONFRONTING BACKLASH STATES"

Foreign Affairs, March/April 1994

A GROUP OF OUTLAWS

The end of the Cold War and the emergence of newly independent states in eastern Europe have the potential to enlarge dramatically the family of nations now committed to the pursuit of democratic institutions, the expansion of free markets, the peaceful settlement of conflict and the promotion of collective security. For the sake of both its interests and its ideals, the United States has a special responsibility to nurture and promote these core values. As the president made clear in his State of the Union address, much of the Clinton administration's foreign policy is devoted to that effort.

At the same time, our policy must face the reality of recalcitrant and outlaw states that not only choose to remain outside the family but also assault its basic values. There are few "backlash" states: Cuba, North Korea, Iran, Iraq and Libya. For now they lack the resources of a superpower, which would enable them to seriously threaten the democratic order being created around them. Nevertheless, their behavior is often aggressive and defiant. The ties between them are growing as they seek to thwart or quarantine themselves from a global trend to which they seem incapable of adapting.

These backlash states have some common characteristics. Ruled by cliques that control power through coercion, they suppress basic human rights and promote radical ideologies. While their political systems vary, their leaders share a common antipathy toward popular participation that might undermine the existing regimes. These nations exhibit a chronic inability to engage constructively with the

---

Anthony Lake was Assistant to the President for National Security Affairs from 1993 to 1997.

outside world, and they do not function effectively in alliances—even with those like-minded. They are often on the defensive, increasingly criticized and targeted with sanctions in international forums.

Finally, they share a siege mentality. Accordingly, they are embarked on ambitious and costly military programs—especially in weapons of mass destruction (WMD) and missile delivery systems—in a misguided quest for a great equalizer to protect their regimes or advance their purposes abroad.

As the sole superpower, the United States has a special responsibility for developing a strategy to neutralize, contain and, through selective pressure, perhaps eventually transform these backlash states into constructive members of the international community. Each backlash state is unique in its history, culture and circumstances, and U.S. strategy has been tailored accordingly. But there are common denominators. In each case, we maintain alliances and deploy military capabilities sufficient to deter or respond to any aggressive act. We seek to contain the influence of these states, sometimes by isolation, sometimes through pressure, sometimes by diplomatic and economic measures. We encourage the rest of the international community to join us in a concerted effort. In the cases of Iraq and Libya, for example, we have already achieved a strong international consensus backed by U.N. resolutions.

The United States is also actively engaged in unilateral and multilateral efforts to restrict their military and technological capabilities. Intelligence, counterterrorism and multilateral export control policies, especially on weapons of mass destruction and their delivery systems, are all being employed. In the North Korean case, for example, its nuclear program is our most urgent concern. The prospect of a nuclear-armed North Korea poses extraordinary risks to our security interests in Asia and the integrity of the global nonproliferation regime. The U.S. military commitment to the security of South Korea is unshakable. America is leading an international effort to persuade North Korea to reverse course. At the same time, we have made it clear to Pyongyang that if it resolves international concerns over its nuclear program, doors will open to better relations. If it does not, however, North Korea will face increased isolation and hardship.

Like North Korea, Iraq and Iran pose serious challenges to our nonproliferation efforts. But because they are located adjacent to each other along the littoral of the vital Persian Gulf, where 65 percent of the world's oil reserves are located, these two backlash states also present a complex strategic puzzle that has confounded the policies of three previous American administrations.

The basic strategic principle in the Persian Gulf region is to establish a favorable balance of power, one that will protect critical American interests in the security of our friends and in the free flow of oil at stable prices. In previous administrations, this was pursued by relying on one regional power to balance the other. First the United States built up Iran under the shah as a supposed regional pillar of stability. Then it backed Saddam Hussein's Iraq in its war with revolutionary Iran to contain the influence of Khomeini's Islamic government. Both approaches proved disastrous. In the shah's case, the U.S. strategy for regional stability collapsed when he was overthrown. And in Saddam Hussein's case, American backing assisted him in acquiring a massive conventional arsenal which he used, first against his own people and then later Kuwait.

THE LOGIC OF DUAL CONTAINMENT

The Clinton administration's strategy toward these two backlash states begins from the premise that today both regimes pursue policies hostile to our interests. Building up one to counter the other is therefore rejected in favor of a policy of "dual containment." In adopting this approach, we are not oblivious to the need for a balance of power in this vital region. Rather, we seek with our regional allies to maintain a favorable balance without depending on either Iraq or Iran. We are able to do so because we have a number of advantages that previous administrations did not.

First, the end of the Cold War simply eliminated a major strategic consideration from our calculus. We no longer have to fear Soviet efforts to gain a foothold in the Persian Gulf by taking advantage of our support for one of these states to build relations with the other. The strategic importance of both Iraq and Iran has therefore been reduced dramatically, and their ability to play the super-powers off each other has been eliminated.

Second, over the last decade, a regional balance of power between Iran and Iraq has been established at a much lower level of military capability. Iraq's victory in the Iran-Iraq War substantially reduced Iran's conventional offensive capabilities. And Iraq's defeat in Desert Storm significantly diminished its offensive capabilities and brought its weapons of mass destruction under tight control. Without the backing of an alternate superpower, they now confront serious difficulties in challenging U.S. power.

Third, as a result of Iraq's invasion of Kuwait, the Gulf Cooperation Council (GCC) states are less reluctant to enter into security and pre-positioning arrangements with Washington. These arrangements provide our military forces with an ability to deploy in the Persian Gulf against any threat that either Iraq or Iran might pose to these states.

Finally, broader trends in the region are positive. Washington enjoys strong relations with the region's other critical powers: Egypt, Israel, Turkey and Saudi Arabia. Progress in resolving the Arab-Israeli conflict solidifies our position in the Arab world and strengthens the ties between our regional allies. It increases the isolation of Iraq and Iran while reducing their ability to exploit the Arab-Israeli conflict to promote their regional ambitions. The comprehensive settlement that the United States seeks will cost Iraq the opportunity to manipulate the Palestinian cause and rob Iran of its ability to promote turmoil in Lebanon.

In sum, until circumstances change there is no longer a need to depend on either Iraq or Iran to maintain a favorable balance and protect U.S. friends and interests in the gulf. The Clinton administration is, nevertheless, confident that we can sustain this situation for some time, in large measure because we have an understanding with our regional friends about the common threats and how to deal with them. While working to consolidate these positive trends, we remain alert to the possibility of change.

"Dual containment" does not mean duplicate containment. The basic purpose is to counter the hostility of both Baghdad and Tehran, but the challenges posed by the two regimes are distinct and therefore require tailored approaches. Although neighbors, the two states are quite different in culture and historical experience. In Saddam Hussein's regime, Washington faces an aggressive, modernist, secular avarice; in Iran, it is challenged by a theocratic regime with a sense of cultural and political destiny and an abiding antagonism toward the United States.

In Iraq, the regime is responsible for both war crimes and crimes against humanity, a regime whose invasion of Kuwait and gassing of its own people have rendered it an international renegade. In post-Khomeini Iran, a revolutionary regime remains engaged in outlaw behavior. Nevertheless, the Clinton administration does not oppose Islamic government, nor does it seek the regime's overthrow. Indeed we remain ready for an authoritative dialogue in which we will raise aspects of Iranian behavior that cause us so much concern.

Containing Iraq presents a different kind of challenge than containing Iran. After the Gulf War, the United Nations established a far-reaching regime to ensure that Iraq never again threatens its neighbors or world peace and to deter Saddam Hussein's aggression against Iraqi citizens. Three years after the invasion of Kuwait, sanctions are still being sustained. The international community is sufficiently alarmed by Saddam's behavior and sufficiently suspicious of his intentions to support Washington's insistence on full compliance with all relevant U.N. Security Council (UNSC) resolutions.

Even today, Saddam's army is engaged in the systematic destruction of the marsh Arab society in southern Iraq while he wages a campaign of terror and blockades against Kurdish, Turkoman and other citizens of northern Iraq. As the Iraqi regime cooperates with the U.N. Special Commission on Iraq (UNSCOM), it is also engaged in clandestine efforts to acquire rocket fuel precursors while failing to give a full accounting of its weapons programs. Thus, it is hardly surprising that every 60 days the sanctions have been extended with little debate.

Lately, Iraq has shown some signs of altering its attitude toward some U.N. requirements, evidenced by its recent acceptance of Security Council Resolution 715, which provides for long-term monitoring of its WMD programs. However, this acceptance comes in the context of continued Iraqi rejection of other Security Council resolutions, especially its refusal to recognize Kuwait's sovereignty and borders. Defiance is thus combined with a guise of compliance. There is plenty of evidence to suggest that the only reason the Iraqi regime is beginning to cooperate with UNSCOM is to secure the lifting of oil sanctions. Once the oil starts flowing again, Washington must assume that Saddam will renege on long-term monitoring and begin rebuilding his WMD programs. Thus, before considering whether oil sanctions are to be lifted, there should be a high degree of confidence that Iraq has not only complied fully with the technical requirements of the WMD provisions but will continue to comply indefinitely. As UNSCOM chairman Rolf Ekeus has insisted, that will require a long period of testing of the permanent monitoring systems. This proposition has been accepted by Washington and its U.N. Security Council (UNSC) partners. They also recognize that the council's review of the sanctions regime will be influenced by Saddam's broader intentions, of which there is ample evidence.

The U.N. resolutions also reflect the international consensus in support of an end to Saddam's repression of the Iraqi people. Working closely with U.N. agencies and international human rights organizations, we are calling attention to the plight of Iraqi citizens who have been brutalized by this regime and insist on having human rights monitors inside the country. The Clinton administration is also engaged directly in humanitarian aid for the Kurds and other groups in northern Iraq as they reconstruct their lives and homes under the protection of coalition forces that deter Saddam's brutality.

The humanitarian efforts of the international community in Iraq are a strong indication of its concern for the plight of the Iraqi people. It is also conscious of the impact of sanctions on their daily lives. Security Council Resolutions 706 and 712—which Saddam refuses to implement—were specifically introduced to alleviate their plight. They would permit Iraq to sell limited quantities of oil to finance the purchase of food and other humanitarian items, provided that the sale and distribution of goods is monitored by the U.N. It should therefore be clear that Saddam Hussein, not the international community, is responsible for their continued suffering.

As a signal of our interest in a democratic Iraq, the Clinton administration also supports the objectives of the Iraqi National Congress, the exile organization that represents a broad spectrum of religious, secular and ethnic communities. The INC has recently broadened its base, established facilities in northern Iraq and deepened its ties with neighboring Arab governments that share the twin goals of maintaining Iraq's territorial integrity while promoting representative and benign governance in Baghdad.

Despite Saddam's efforts to buy loyalties, sanctions are taking their toll on the crucial inner circle on which the regime depends. There are now frequent reports of coup attempts and unrest among the relatively privileged Iraqi elite. These trends could lead to new conditions for the citizens of Iraq and new opportunities to build a more peaceful and normal relationship between Iraq and the outside world.

THE CHALLENGE FROM TEHRAN

Iran is both a lesser and a greater challenge. On the one hand, the Clinton administration is not confronting a blatantly aggressive state that invaded and occupied a weaker neighbor. More normal relations with the government in Tehran are conceivable, once it demonstrates its willingness to abide by international norms and abandon policies and actions inimical to regional peace and security. On the other hand, political differences with Iran will not easily be resolved. Iran is a revolutionary state whose leaders harbor a deep sense of grievance over the close ties between the United States and the shah. Its revolutionary and militant messages are openly hostile to the United States and its core interests. This basic political reality will shape relations for the foreseeable future. Reconciliation will be difficult, but the choice is Iran's to make.

The American quarrel with Iran should not be misconstrued as a "clash of civilizations" or opposition to Iran as a theocratic state. Washington does not take issue with the "Islamic" dimension of the Islamic Republic of Iran. As President Clinton has said, America has a deep respect for the religion and culture of Islam. It is extremism, whether religious or secular, that we oppose. The United States is concerned with the actions and policies of the Tehran government. Iran is actively engaged in clandestine efforts to acquire nuclear and other unconventional weapons and long-range missile-delivery systems. It is the foremost sponsor of terrorism and assassination worldwide. It is violently and vitriolically opposed to the Arab-Israeli peace process. It seeks to subvert friendly governments across the Middle East and in parts of Africa. It is attempting to acquire offensive conventional capabilities to threaten its smaller gulf neighbors. Its record on treatment of its own citizens—especially women and religious minorities—is deeply disturbing.

In confronting these manifold challenges, the Clinton administration faces an easier task than in the case of Iraq because Iran's weapons of mass destruction are at a relatively early stage of development. In that sense it has an opportunity now to prevent Iran from becoming in five years time what Iraq was five years ago. But containment is also more difficult because the administration is not backed by an international consensus reflected in UNSC resolutions, as in Iraq's case. And it does not have broad sanctions in place to effect changes in Iran's unacceptable behavior. Previous administrations have tried their hands at building up "moderates" in Iran. What we have learned from that experience is that these same "moderates" are responsible for the very policies we find so objectionable. However, Iran's economic mismanagement has combined with the downturn in the oil market to produce a desperate economic situation for the Iranian government. With 30 percent inflation, a $30 billion debt and $5 billion in arrears on its short-term repayments, Iran no longer looks like a good commercial proposition. This makes it easier to argue with U.S. allies against improving ties with Iran for purely commercial motives.

To counter Iran's quest for domination of the Persian Gulf, Washington works closely with friendly governments to prevent Iran from procuring needed imports for its nuclear and chemical programs, and is vigilant about the transfer of missiles and missile-related systems from Iran's current suppliers, including North Korea. This does not mean Washington intends to quarantine Iran or deny it all military-related goods. This administration tries to distinguish between defense items that do not affect the regional security environment and those items that have an offensive use and could destabilize the area.

NOT A CRUSADE BUT A COMMITMENT

The U.S. strategy depends heavily on active coordination and consultations with friendly countries. Iran needs to hear a steady and consistent message from the Western countries whose approval and trade it seeks. We have achieved some consensus among the European Union, Canada and Japan on those aspects of Iran's actions that we find unacceptable. Some of our allies believe, however, that the regional policy must rely largely on positive incentives for Iran. The record clearly shows, however, that positive inducements such as trade and aid concessions or rescheduling of loans do not lead to real changes in Iran's unacceptable behavior. The most effective message is a consistent one: no normal relations until these actions end. But we do not eschew an authoritative dialogue; dialogue and pressure are not mutually exclusive policy approaches.

There are some risks inherent in the coupling of our approaches to Iraq and Iran. To the extent they are pressured, they may be driven together in their efforts to resist the West. Indeed, Baghdad and Tehran seem to have engaged in limited cooperation over the past year, despite their differences. Ultimately, however, the prospects for reconciliation will remain limited for a simple reason: they mistrust each other more than they mistrust the United States. While they have a common interest in tactical cooperation, neither has a real interest in helping the other grow stronger; each knows that it will be the first target of a resurgent state on the other side of the Shatt-al-Arab.

There is also the danger that in maintaining our efforts to force Iraq to comply with all U.N. resolutions, we will provide opportunities for Iran to meddle and prey on Iraqi weakness. Again, we have seen efforts by Iran to build its relations with Iraq's Shiites and meddle in Kurdish politics. But the evidence suggests this fear is exaggerated. From the time of the Iran-Iraq war, Iraq's Shiites have retained their Iraqi and Arab identity and remain wary of falling under Iran's influence. Similarly, Iran's efforts in the north seem focused on weakening its own separatist Kurdish minority rather than seeking to weaken Iraq by promoting the breakaway of the north. Indeed, like Iraq's other neighbors, Syria and Turkey, Iran seems concerned to avoid the disintegration of Iraq for fear that it will encourage the disintegration of its own hinterland.

The Clinton administration has forged a realistic and sustainable policy that takes into account U.S. interests and the realities of the Persian Gulf region. Today the regimes in Baghdad and Tehran are weaker and increasingly on the defensive. Slowly but surely they are coming to understand that there is a price to pay for their recalcitrant commitment to remain on the wrong side of history. This is not a crusade, but a genuine and responsible effort, over time, to protect American strategic interests, stabilize the international system and enlarge the community of nations committed to democracy, free markets and peace.

Forty-seven years ago, George Kennan, writing under a pseudonym in this journal, made the case for containment of an outlaw empire. He argued that the United States had within its power the means to "to increase enormously the strains under which Soviet policy must operate" and thereby generate the "break-up or gradual mellowing of Soviet power." Today, the United States faces a less formidable challenge in containing the band of outlaws we refer to as "the backlash states." It is still very much within our power to prevail.

SECRETARY OF STATE MADELEINE K. ALBRIGHT, "PRESERVING PRINCIPLE AND SAFEGUARDING STABILITY: UNITED STATES POLICY TOWARD IRAQ"

Excerpts from Remarks at Georgetown University, Washington, D.C., March 26, 1997

My fundamental purpose is to reaffirm United States policy towards Iraq. That policy is part of a broad commitment to protect the security and territory of our friends and allies in the Gulf. We have a vital national interest in the security of the region's oil supplies, and we have forged strong friendships with countries in the area who agree with us that nations should respect international law, refrain from aggression and oppose those who commit or sponsor terror.

Here, as elsewhere, we recognize that stability is not an import; it must be home-grown. But we also know that circumstances may arise in which active American leadership and power are required.

A compelling example was Iraq's invasion of Kuwait six and a half years ago.

The results of that event remain with us now. So before discussing where we go from here in our policy towards Iraq, let me review how we got to where we are.

When President Bush launched Operation Desert Storm, he said that America had two objectives. First, to drive Iraq out of Kuwait. Second, to cause Iraq once again to "live as a peaceful and cooperative member of the family of nations."

Because of the bravery and brilliance of the U.S.-led military coalition, the first objective was quickly achieved.

But despite the lessons of war, continuing international pressure, the impact of tough U.N. sanctions, and the best interests of the Iraqi people, Iraq's government has continued to defy the will of the international community.

Under resolutions approved by the U.N. Security Council, Iraq is required to demonstrate its peaceful intentions by meeting a series of obligations. It must end its weapons of mass destruction programs and destroy any such weapons produced. It must cooperate with the inspection and monitoring regime established by the U.N. Special Commission, or UNSCOM. And it must recognize its border with Kuwait, return stolen property, account for POW/MIAs, end support for terrorism and stop brutalizing its people.

Had Iraq complied with these obligations early on, its economy would have recovered, the oil trade would have resumed, debts would have been paid, the suffering of its people would have been avoided, and it could have resumed its rightful place among the responsible nations of the world.

Instead, from the outset, Iraqi leaders chose denial, delay and deceit. Or to put it even more bluntly, they lied.

They have blocked inspections, concealed documents, falsified evidence and challenged UNSCOM's clear and legitimate authority.

They have refused to account satisfactorily for Kuwaiti missing and prisoners of war.

They have failed to return stolen property and weapons.

They have virtually demolished the marsh Arab community in southern Iraq, waged war on the minorities in the north and accelerated repression in the center to stay in power.

And their agents have crossed borders to gun down or poison Iraqi dissidents.

Throughout, their leader, Saddam Hussein, has bemoaned the unfairness of sanctions and the indignity of inspections.

His complaints remind me of the story about the schoolboy who returned home with his nose bloodied and his shirt torn. When his mother asked him how the fight started, he said "it started when the other guy hit me back."

Since 1991, the task of looking behind Iraqi deceptions to find the truth has fallen to the IAEA and to UNSCOM Chairman Rolf Ekeus and his staff.

For years, they have struggled to discover and destroy Iraq's once extensive arsenal of weapons of mass destruction. Although they have been harassed and threatened by Iraqi officials, they have made steady—and at times stunning—progress.

The defection in 1995 of Hussein Kamil, the official who directed many of Iraq's efforts at deception, marked a turning point. It led to major revelations regarding biological weapons and appeared, for a time, as if it would cause Iraq finally to accept the need for full disclosure.

Unfortunately, this has not been the case. The refusal to cooperate fully continued throughout 1996 and to the present time.

This tactic has not and will not work.

Our resolve on this point is unwavering. Hundreds of thousands of American soldiers put their lives on the line in the Gulf War. We will not allow Iraq to regain by stonewalling the Security Council what it forfeited by aggression on the battlefield.

We know from experience that firmness is the only language the Iraqi Government understands. In 1993, when Iraq plotted the assassination of former President Bush, the United States struck back hard.

In 1994, when Iraqi troops again threatened Kuwait, President Clinton's firm military and diplomatic response caused Baghdad not only to pull back its troops, but to recognize—at long last—its legal border with Kuwait. Moreover, a new Security Council Resolution restricted military activity in southern Iraq.

Last August, Iraqi forces took advantage of intra-Kurdish tensions and attacked the city of Irbil, in northern Iraq. President Clinton responded by expanding the no-fly zone to the southern suburbs of Baghdad. This reduced further the strategic threat posed by Iraq and demonstrated our intention to respond to Iraqi transgressions in a manner of our choosing.

Contrary to some expectations, the attack on Irbil has not restored Saddam Hussein's authority in the north. Iraqi troops have withdrawn from Irbil, and the region's inhabitants, conscious of Baghdad's past repression against them, have resisted efforts by the regime to re-establish control.

The Kurdish parties have been working with us to limit their differences and seek common ground. Although old rivalries remain difficult, we are firmly engaged alongside Turkey and the United

Kingdom in helping the inhabitants of the region find stability and work towards a unified and pluralistic Iraq.

Although we oppose the lawless policies of the Iraqi regime, we have never had a quarrel with the Iraqi people. U.N. sanctions do not prohibit food and medical supplies. But because Saddam Hussein did not use his resources to meet the basic needs of his people, we supported efforts for additional relief.

For five years, Baghdad refused to accept such an arrangement. It was not until late last year that Iraq finally caved in to international pressure and agreed.

The food for oil deal now in place is designed to ease the suffering of civilians throughout Iraq. It is not related to the larger question of when and if the overall sanctions regime will be lifted. Nor is the continuation of this arrangement automatic, however strongly we support its purpose. If we see evidence that the Government of Iraq is not living up to its promises with respect to implementation, the experiment will cease.

All this brings us to the present day. From the beginning of Operation Desert Storm until now, American policy towards Iraq has been consistent, principled and grounded in a realistic and hard-won understanding of the nature of the Iraqi regime. It has been bolstered by bipartisan support at home, and general approval in the region. And it has achieved a great deal.

Iraq's military threat to its neighbors is greatly diminished.

Most of its missiles have been destroyed.

Its biological and chemical warfare production facilities have been dismantled.

Nuclear materials have been removed and an international monitoring regime to prevent the construction of nuclear weapons is in place.

Iraq has been barred from importing weapons and weapons-related materials and technology.

And the area in which Iraqi military forces may operate freely has contracted.

To guard against further miscalculations on Baghdad's part, U.S. forces have been deployed to the region and we have demonstrated our ability to reinforce those troops rapidly if required.

Diplomatically, we have sustained an international consensus that Iraq should not be allowed again to threaten international peace. In statement after statement, and in 36 successive reviews, the Security Council has maintained its support for sanctions and its insistence on compliance.

Meanwhile, six years of sanctions and isolation have taken their toll on the regime in Baghdad. Saddam Hussein has become by far the most divisive force in Iraq, and several coup attempts have been made. Members of his own somewhat dysfunctional family have turned against him. His inner circle of advisers has been purged repeatedly. Today, his power rests on an increasingly narrow foundation of intimidation and terror.

So while Iraq's lawless policies are failing, our policies of law and firmness are working. As long as the apparatus of sanctions, enforcement, inspections and monitoring is in place, Iraq will remain trapped within a strategic box, unable to successfully threaten its neighbors and unable to realize the grandiose ambitions of its ignoble leader.

It is essential, however, that international resolve not weaken. Containment has worked, but—despite Iraq's present weakness—the future threat has not been erased. Iraq's behavior and intentions must change before our policies can change. Otherwise, we will allow the scorpion that bit us once to bite us again. That would be a folly impossible to explain to our children, or to the veterans of Desert Storm.

Consider that, under Saddam Hussein, Iraq has started two major wars, used poison gas and committed gross violations of international humanitarian law.

Consider that Iraq admitted producing chemical and biological warfare agents before the Gulf War that were sufficiently lethal to kill every man, woman and child on earth.

Consider that Iraq has yet to provide convincing evidence that it has destroyed all of these weapons.

Consider that Iraq admitted loading many of those agents into missile warheads before the war.

Consider that Iraq retains more than 7500 nuclear scientists and technicians, as well as technical documents related to the production of nuclear weapons.

Consider that Iraq has been caught trying to smuggle in missile guidance instruments.

And consider that, according to Ambassador Ekeus, UNSCOM has not been able to account for all the missiles Iraq acquired over the years. In fact, Ekeus believes it is highly likely that Iraq retains an operational SCUD missile force, probably with chemical or biological weapons to go with it.

If past is prologue, under the current government, an Iraq released from sanctions and scrutiny would pick up where it left off a half dozen years ago—before the mother of all coalitions stopped it dead in its tracks.

For these reasons, our policy will not change. It is the right policy.

To those who ask how long our determination will last; how long we will oppose Iraqi intransigence; how long we will insist that the international community's standards be met, our answer is—as long as it takes.

We do not agree with the nations who argue that if Iraq complies with its obligations concerning weapons of mass destruction, sanctions should be lifted. Our view, which is unshakable, is that Iraq must prove its peaceful intentions. It can only do that by complying with all of the Security Council Resolutions to which it is subject.

Is it possible to conceive of such a government under Saddam Hussein? When I was a professor, I taught that you have to consider all possibilities. As Secretary of State, I have to deal in the realm of reality and probability. And the evidence is overwhelming that Saddam Hussein's intentions will never be peaceful.

The United States looks forward, nevertheless, to the day when Iraq rejoins the family of nations as a responsible and law abiding member. This is in our interests and in the interests of our allies and partners within the region.

Clearly, a change in Iraq's government could lead to a change in U.S. policy. Should that occur, we would stand ready, in coordination with our allies and friends, to enter rapidly into a dialogue with the successor regime.

That dialogue would have two principal goals.

First, because we are firmly committed to Iraq's territorial integrity, we would want to verify that the new Iraq would be independent, unified and free from undue external influence for example, from Iran.

Second, we would require improvements in behavior. Is there cooperation with UNSCOM and compliance with U.N. resolutions? Is there respect for human rights, including the rights of minorities? Is there a convincing repudiation of terrorism? Are its military ambitions limited to those of reasonable defense?

If our concerns were addressed satisfactorily, Iraq would no longer threaten regional security. Its isolation could end.

The international community, including the United States, would look for ways to ease Iraq's re-integration. A whole range of economic and security matters would be open for discussion in a climate of cooperation and mutual respect. Iraq could begin to reclaim its potential as a nation rich in resources and blessed by a talented and industrious people. And Iraq could become a pillar of peace and stability in the region.

But until that day comes, we must—and will—maintain our watch.

We will continue to work closely with our allies and friends to ensure that Iraq does not again attack its neighbors or put them at risk.

We will retain in the region the military capability required to deter Iraqi aggression and to enforce the no-fly and no-drive zones.

We will maintain a firm commitment to the territorial sovereignty of Kuwait and our other friends in the region.

We will lend our full diplomatic support to the work of the U.N. Special Commission and the International Atomic Energy Agency.

We will insist, with all of the diplomatic tools at our command, that U.N. sanctions remain in place. Within that context, we will do what we responsibly can to minimize the suffering of Iraqi citizens.

We will continue to support the establishment of a coherent and united Iraqi opposition which represents the country's ethnic and confessional diversity.

And we will continue helping the people of northern Iraq to meet their practical needs, resolve internal tensions, and reject the influence of terrorists.

The Baghdad of 1200 years ago was described as the center of "a properly regulated and well ordered" state, "where schools and colleges abound, (to which) philosophers, students, doctors and priests . . . flock . . . (and where) the governors and ministers (are) honest."

Clearly, Saddam Hussein has not been an agent of progress.

And clearly, what is now need not always be.

The rip in the fabric of Gulf stability that was created by Iraq's invasion of Kuwait has not fully mended. But the aggression has been rolled back. Iraq's military is contained. And the path for Iraq's re-entry into the community of nations is clearly laid out.

This is not, to borrow Margaret Thatcher's phrase, the time to go wobbly towards Iraq.

The United States is committed—as are our friends—to the victory of principle over expediency; and to the evolution in Iraq of a society based on law, exemplified by pluralism and content to live at peace.

These goals may be achieved soon.

They may be achieved not-so-soon.

But they are right; they are necessary; and they will be achieved.

Thank you very much.

QUESTIONS

Question: This question concerns the future strategic and territorial arrangements of Iraq. From time to time, pundits have joined, or voiced the idea of dismembering Iraq. By saying to them, aren't we doing Saddam Hussein a favor? I think the implication of the question is, should we be moving to keep Iraq territorially intact?

Secretary Albright: We have believed consistently that it is very important to maintain the territorial integrity of Iraq. It is important for the stability of the region. It is important for the people of Iraq. But the point is to make sure that the variety of people that live in Iraq, in the north, center, and south, are able, in fact, to have the appropriate liberties that are required of countries that have a number of minorities and not to have the kinds of repression of people that Saddam Hussein has exerted both in the north and in the south where he has, basically, in the south, destroyed a whole system of living that the people there have had.

We do believe that it is important for the stability of the region to keep repeating and also keep insisting that there be the territorial integrity of Iraq.

Question: The next question concerns the sanction regimes and not only its future but are there going to be alternatives to a sanctions regime in order to keep Iraq both militarily contained and politically stable?

Secretary Albright: Beyond the sanctions?

Question: Beyond the sanctions.

Secretary Albright: Let me just say something about the sanctions regime themselves. Having participated at many of those reviews that I've discussed, there was always the issue as to what the sanctions regime had accomplished. I think that what is important to know is, for instance, the work that Chairman Ekeus has undertaken through UNSCOM and then with IAEA has brought about the following results.

In the chemical weapons area, there has been the destruction of 28,000 chemical munitions, 480,000 liters of chemical weapons agents, 1.8 million liters and over 1 million kilograms of 45 different precursor chemicals, and a variety of biological weapon production equipment.

In the biological area, the entire Al-Hakam custom-built biological weapon factory complex has been dismantled and a huge variety of biological weapon production equipment has also been removed.

In the nuclear area, all quantities of special nuclear material—that is, highly enriched uranium or plutonium—found in Iraq have been removed, and the industrial infrastructure which Iraq has set up to produce and weaponize special nuclear materials has been destroyed. So I think that we should understand that the sanctions regime has in fact been quite successful and needs to remain in place.

What is important here for us to say, and as I said in my remarks, is that we are prepared to have a dialogue with a successor regime that does in fact abide by what was required as a result of the Gulf War, and that is the policy that one needs to look towards: that the sanctions regime is working, the coalition is firm, and the firmness of the Security Council and the coalition is what is going to keep this on track. But, as I said, we are prepared to deal with a successor.

Question: This question concerns the relations between the United States and a neighbor country. What do you foresee, if any, changes in U.S. relations with Iran would have to be in the continuing effort to contain Iraq?

Secretary Albright: We, as you know, have had a policy of dual containment. We believe that that policy is an appropriate one, and that it is important in fact for the stability of the region to make sure that Iran is also not involved in creation of weapons of mass destruction, support for the peace process, and does not support terrorism. Therefore, we consider that our policies as far as Iran and Iraq are concerned are the right policies, and we will pursue them in that vein.

U.S. PUBLIC LAW 104–172: THE IRAN AND LIBYA SANCTIONS ACT OF 1996

Excerpts with Respect to Iran

An Act to impose sanctions on persons making certain investments directly and significantly contributing to the enhancement of the ability of Iran or Libya to develop its petroleum resources ...

SECTION 1. SHORT TITLE.

This Act may be cited as the "Iran and Libya Sanctions Act of 1996."

SEC. 2. FINDINGS.

The Congress makes the following findings:

(1) The efforts of the Government of Iran to acquire weapons of mass destruction and the means to deliver them and its support of acts of international terrorism endanger the national security and foreign policy interests of the United States and those countries with which the United States shares common strategic and foreign policy objectives.

(2) The objective of preventing the proliferation of weapons of mass destruction and acts of international terrorism through existing multilateral and bilateral initiatives requires additional efforts to deny Iran the financial means to sustain its nuclear, chemical, biological, and missile weapons programs.

(3) The Government of Iran uses its diplomatic facilities and quasi-governmental institutions outside of Iran to promote acts of international terrorism and assist its nuclear, chemical, biological, and missile weapons programs.

SEC. 3. DECLARATION OF POLICY.

(a) POLICY WITH RESPECT TO IRAN.—The Congress declares that it is the policy of the United States to deny Iran the ability to support acts of international terrorism and to fund the development and acquisition of weapons of mass destruction and the means to deliver them by limiting the development of Iran's ability to explore for, extract, refine, or transport by pipeline petroleum resources of Iran.

SEC. 4. MULTILATERAL REGIME.

(a) MULTILATERAL NEGOTIATIONS.—In order to further the objectives of section 3, the Congress urges the President to commence immediately diplomatic efforts, both in appropriate international fora such as the United Nations, and bilaterally with allies of the United States, to establish a multilateral sanctions regime against Iran, including provisions limiting the development of petroleum resources, that will inhibit Iran's efforts to carry out activities described in section 2.

(b) REPORTS TO CONGRESS.—The President shall report to the appropriate congressional committees, not later than 1 year after the date of the enactment of this Act, and periodically thereafter, on the extent that diplomatic efforts described in subsection (a) have been successful. Each report shall include—

 (1) the countries that have agreed to undertake measures to further the objectives of section 3 with respect to Iran, and a description of those measures; and

 (2) the countries that have not agreed to measures described in paragraph (1), and, with respect to those countries, other measures (in addition to that provided in subsection (d)) the President recommends that the United States take to further the objectives of section 3 with respect to Iran.

(c) WAIVER.—The President may waive the application of section 5(a) with respect to nationals of a country if—

 (1) that country has agreed to undertake substantial measures, including economic sanctions, that will inhibit Iran's efforts

to carry out activities described in section 2 and information required by subsection (b)(1) has been included in a report submitted under subsection (b); and

(2) the President, at least 30 days before the waiver takes effect, notifies the appropriate congressional committees of his intention to exercise the waiver.

(d) ENHANCED SANCTION.—

(1) SANCTION.—With respect to nationals of countries except those with respect to which the President has exercised the waiver authority of subsection (c), at any time after the first report is required to be submitted under subsection (b), section 5(a) shall be applied by substituting "$20,000,000" for "$40,000,000" each place it appears, and by substituting "$5,000,000" for "$10,000,000."

(2) REPORT TO CONGRESS.—The President shall report to the appropriate congressional committees any country with respect to which paragraph (1) applies.

(e) INTERIM REPORT ON MULTILATERAL SANCTIONS; MONITORING.—The President, not later than 90 days after the date of the enactment of this Act, shall report to the appropriate congressional committees on—

(1) whether the member states of the European Union, the Republic of Korea, Australia, Israel, or Japan have legislative or administrative standards providing for the imposition of trade sanctions on persons or their affiliates doing business or having investments in Iran or Libya;

(2) the extent and duration of each instance of the application of such sanctions; and

(3) the disposition of any decision with respect to such sanctions by the World Trade Organization or its predecessor organization.

SEC. 5. IMPOSITION OF SANCTIONS.

(a) SANCTIONS WITH RESPECT TO IRAN.—Except as provided in subsection (f), the President shall impose 2 or more of the sanctions described in paragraphs (1) through (6) of section 6 if the

President determines that a person has, with actual knowledge, on or after the date of the enactment of this Act, made an investment of $40,000,000 or more (or any combination of investments of at least $10,000,000 each, which in the aggregate equals or exceeds $40,000,000 in any 12-month period), that directly and significantly contributed to the enhancement of Iran's ability to develop petroleum resources of Iran.

(c) PERSONS AGAINST WHICH THE SANCTIONS ARE TO BE IMPOSED.—The sanctions described in subsections (a) and (b) shall be imposed on—

> (1) any person the President determines has carried out the activities described in subsection (a) or (h); and
> (2) any person the President determines—
>> (A) is a successor entity to the person referred to in paragraph (1);
>> (B) is a parent or subsidiary of the person referred to in paragraph (1) if that parent or subsidiary, with actual knowledge, engaged in the activities referred to in paragraph (1); or
>> (C) is an affiliate of the person referred to in paragraph (1) if that affiliate, with actual knowledge, engaged in the activities referred to in paragraph (1) and if that affiliate is controlled in fact by the person referred to in paragraph (1).

For purposes of this Act, any person or entity described in this subsection shall be referred to as a "sanctioned person."

(d) PUBLICATION IN FEDERAL REGISTER.—The President shall cause to be published in the Federal Register a current list of persons and entities on whom sanctions have been imposed under this Act. The removal of persons or entities from, and the addition of persons and entities to, the list, shall also be so published.

(e) PUBLICATION OF PROJECTS.—The President shall cause to be published in the Federal Register a list of all significant projects which have been publicly tendered in the oil and gas sector in Iran.

(f) EXCEPTIONS.—The President shall not be required to apply or maintain the sanctions under subsection (a) or (b)—

(1) in the case of procurement of defense articles or defense services—

(A) under existing contracts or subcontracts, including the exercise of options for production quantities to satisfy requirements essential to the national security of the United States;

(B) if the President determines in writing that the person to which the sanctions would otherwise be applied is a sole source supplier of the defense articles or services, that the defense articles or services are essential, and that alternative sources are not readily or reasonably available; or

(C) if the President determines in writing that such articles or services are essential to the national security under defense coproduction agreements;

(2) in the case of procurement, to eligible products, as defined in section 308(4) of the Trade Agreements Act of 1979 (19 U.S.C. 2515(4)), of any foreign country or instrumentality designated under section 301(b)(1) of that Act (19 U.S.C. 2511(b)(1));

(3) to products, technology, or services provided under contracts entered into before the date on which the President publishes in the Federal Register the name of the person on whom the sanctions are to be imposed;

(4) to—

(A) spare parts which are essential to United States products or production;

(B) component parts, but not finished products, essential to United States products or production; or

(C) routine servicing and maintenance of products, to the extent that alternative sources are not readily or reasonably available;

(6) to information and technology essential to United States products or production; or

(7) to medicines, medical supplies, or other humanitarian items.

SEC. 6. DESCRIPTION OF SANCTIONS.

The sanctions to be imposed on a sanctioned person under section 5 are as follows:

(1) EXPORT-IMPORT BANK ASSISTANCE FOR EXPORTS TO SANCTIONED PERSONS.—The President may direct the Export-Import Bank of the United States not to give approval to the issuance of any guarantee, insurance, extension of credit, or participation in the extension of credit in connection with the export of any goods or services to any sanctioned person.

(2) EXPORT SANCTION.—The President may order the United States Government not to issue any specific license and not to grant any other specific permission or authority to export any goods or technology to a sanctioned person under—

(i) the Export Administration Act of 1979;

(ii) the Arms Expert Control Act;

(iii) the Atomic Energy Act of 1954; or

(iv) any other statute that requires the prior review and approval of the United States Government as a condition for the export or reexport of goods or services.

(3) LOANS FROM UNITED STATES FINANCIAL INSTITUTIONS.—The United States Government may prohibit any United States financial institution from making loans or providing credits to any sanctioned person totaling more than $10,000,000 in any 12-month period unless such person is engaged in activities to relieve human suffering and the loans or credits are provided for such activities.

(4) PROHIBITIONS ON FINANCIAL INSTITUTIONS.—The following prohibitions may be imposed against a sanctioned person that is a financial institution:

(A) PROHIBITION ON DESIGNATION AS PRIMARY DEALER.—Neither the Board of Governors of the Federal Reserve System nor the Federal Reserve Bank of New York may designate, or permit the continuation of any prior designation of, such financial institution as a primary dealer in United States Government debt instruments.

(B) PROHIBITION ON SERVICE AS A REPOSITORY OF GOVERNMENT FUNDS.—Such financial institution may not serve as agent of the United States Government or serve as repository for United States Government funds.

The imposition of either sanction under subparagraph (A) or (B) shall be treated as 1 sanction for purposes of section 5, and the imposition of both such sanctions shall be treated as 2 sanctions for purposes of section 5.

(5) PROCUREMENT SANCTION.—The United States Government may not procure, or enter into any contract for the procurement of, any goods or services from a sanctioned person.

(6) ADDITIONAL SANCTIONS.—The President may impose sanctions, as appropriate, to restrict imports with respect to a sanctioned person, in accordance with the International Emergency Economic Powers Act (50 U.S.C. 1701 and following).

SEC. 7. ADVISORY OPINIONS.

The Secretary of State may, upon the request of any person, issue an advisory opinion to that person as to whether a proposed activity by that person would subject that person to sanctions under this Act. Any person who relies in good faith on such an advisory opinion which states that the proposed activity would not subject a person to such sanctions, and any person who thereafter engages in such activity, will not be made subject to such sanctions on account of such activity.

SEC. 8. TERMINATION OF SANCTIONS.

(a) IRAN.—The requirement under section 5(a) to impose sanctions shall no longer have force or effect with respect to Iran if the President determines and certifies to the appropriate congressional committees that Iran—

(1) has ceased its efforts to design, develop, manufacture, or acquire—

    (A) a nuclear explosive device or related materials and technology;

    (B) chemical and biological weapons; and

    (C) ballistic missiles and ballistic missile launch technology; and

(2) has been removed from the list of countries the governments of which have been determined, for purposes of section 6(j) of the Export Administration Act of 1979, to have repeatedly provided support for acts of international terrorism.

SEC. 9. DURATION OF SANCTIONS; PRESIDENTIAL WAIVER.

(a) DELAY OF SANCTIONS.—

    (1) CONSULTATIONS.—If the President makes a determination described in section 5(a) or 5(b) with respect to a foreign person, the Congress urges the President to initiate consultations immediately with the government with primary jurisdiction over that foreign person with respect to the imposition of sanctions under this Act.

    (2) ACTIONS BY GOVERNMENT OF JURISDICTION.—In order to pursue consultations under paragraph (1) with the government concerned, the President may delay imposition of sanctions under this Act for up to 90 days. Following such consultations, the President shall immediately impose sanctions unless the President determines and certifies to the Congress that the government has taken specific and effective actions, including, as appropriate, the imposition of appropriate penalties, to terminate the involvement of the foreign person in the activities that resulted in the determination by the President under section 5(a) or 5(b) concerning such person.

    3) ADDITIONAL DELAY IN IMPOSITION OF SANCTIONS.—The President may delay the imposition of sanctions for up to an additional 90 days if the President

determines and certifies to the Congress that the government with primary jurisdiction over the person concerned is in the process of taking the actions described in paragraph (2).

(4) REPORT TO CONGRESS.—Not later than 90 days after making a determination under section 5(a) or 5(b), the President shall submit to the appropriate congressional committees a report on the status of consultations with the appropriate foreign government under this subsection, and the basis for any determination under paragraph (3).

(b) DURATION OF SANCTIONS.—A sanction imposed under section 5 shall remain in effect—

(1) for a period of not less than 2 years from the date on which it is imposed; or

(2) until such time as the President determines and certifies to the Congress that the person whose activities were the basis for imposing the sanction is no longer engaging in such activities and that the President has received reliable assurances that such person will not knowingly engage in such activities in the future, except that such sanction shall remain in effect for a period of at least 1 year.

(c) PRESIDENTIAL WAIVER.—

(1) AUTHORITY.—The President may waive the requirement in section 5 to impose a sanction or sanctions on a person described in section 5(c), and may waive the continued imposition of a sanction or sanctions under subsection (b) of this section, 30 days or more after the President determines and so reports to the appropriate congressional committees that it is important to the national interest of the United States to exercise such waiver authority.

(2) CONTENTS OF REPORT.—Any report under paragraph (1) shall provide a specific and detailed rationale for the determination under paragraph (1), including—

(A) a description of the conduct that resulted in the determination under section 5(a) or (b), as the case may be;

(B) in the case of a foreign person, an explanation of

the efforts to secure the cooperation of the government with primary jurisdiction over the sanctioned person to terminate or, as appropriate, penalize the activities that resulted in the determination under section 5(a) or (b), as the case may be;

(C) an estimate as to the significance—

(i) of the provision of the items described in section 5(a) to Iran's ability to develop its petroleum resources, or

(3) EFFECT OF REPORT ON WAIVER.—If the President makes a report under paragraph (1) with respect to a waiver of sanctions on a person described in section 5(c), sanctions need not be imposed under section 5(a) or (b) on that person during the 30-day period referred to in paragraph (1).

SEC. 10. REPORTS REQUIRED.

(a) REPORT ON CERTAIN INTERNATIONAL INITIATIVES.—Not later than 6 months after the date of the enactment of this Act, and every 6 months thereafter, the President shall transmit a report to the appropriate congressional committees describing—

(1) the efforts of the President to mount a multilateral campaign to persuade all countries to pressure Iran to cease its nuclear, chemical, biological, and missile weapons programs and its support of acts of international terrorism;

(2) the efforts of the President to persuade other governments to ask Iran to reduce the presence of Iranian diplomats and representatives of other government and military or quasi-governmental institutions of Iran and to withdraw any such diplomats or representatives who participated in the takeover of the United States embassy in Tehran on November 4, 1979, or the subsequent holding of United States hostages for 444 days;

(3) the extent to which the International Atomic Energy Agency has established regular inspections of all nuclear facilities in Iran, including those presently under construction; and

(4) Iran's use of Iranian diplomats and representatives of other government and military or quasi-governmental institutions of Iran to promote acts of international terrorism or to develop or sustain Iran's nuclear, chemical, biological, and missile weapons programs.

(b) OTHER REPORTS.—The President shall ensure the continued transmittal to the Congress of reports describing—
(1) the nuclear and other military capabilities of Iran, as required by section 601(a) of the Nuclear Non-Proliferation Act of 1978 and section 1607 of the National Defense Authorization Act for Fiscal Year 1993; and
(2) the support provided by Iran for acts of international terrorism, as part of the Department of State's annual report on international terrorism.

SEC. 11. DETERMINATIONS NOT REVIEWABLE.

A determination to impose sanctions under this Act shall not be reviewable in any court.

SEC. 12. EXCLUSION OF CERTAIN ACTIVITIES.

Nothing in this Act shall apply to any activities subject to the reporting requirements of title V of the National Security Act of 1947.

SEC. 13. EFFECTIVE DATE; SUNSET.

(a) EFFECTIVE DATE.—This Act shall take effect on the date of the enactment of this Act.

(b) SUNSET.—This Act shall cease to be effective on the date that is 5 years after the date of the enactment of this Act.

SEC. 14. DEFINITIONS.
As used in this Act:
(1) ACT OF INTERNATIONAL TERRORISM.—The term "act of international terrorism" means an act—
(A) which is violent or dangerous to human life and that

is a violation of the criminal laws of the United States or of any State or that would be a criminal violation if committed within the jurisdiction of the United States or any State; and

(B) which appears to be intended—

(i) to intimidate or coerce a civilian population;

(ii) to influence the policy of a government by intimidation or coercion; or

(iii) to affect the conduct of a government by assassination or kidnapping.

(2) APPROPRIATE CONGRESSIONAL COMMITTEES.—The term "appropriate congressional committees" means the Committee on Finance, the Committee on Banking, Housing, and Urban Affairs, and the Committee on Foreign Relations of the Senate and the Committee on Ways and Means, the Committee on Banking and Financial Services, and the Committee on International Relations of the House of Representatives.

(3) COMPONENT PART.—The term "component part" has the meaning given that term in section 11A(e)(1) of the Expert Administration Act of 1979 (50 U.S.C. App. 2410a(e)(1)).

(4) DEVELOP AND DEVELOPMENT.—To "develop," or the "development" of, petroleum resources means the exploration for, or the extraction, refining, or transportation by pipeline of, petroleum resources.

(5) FINANCIAL INSTITUTION.—The term "financial institution" includes—

(A) a depository institution (as defined in section 3(c)(1) of the Federal Deposit Insurance Act), including a branch or agency of a foreign bank (as defined in section 1(b)(7) of the International Banking Act of 1978);

(B) a credit union;

(C) a securities firm, including a broker or dealer;

(D) an insurance company, including an agency or underwriter; and

(E) any other company that provides financial services.

(6) FINISHED PRODUCT.—The term "finished product" has the meaning given that term in section 11A(e)(2) of the Export Administration Act of 1979 (50 U.S.C. App. 2410a(e)(2))

(7) FOREIGN PERSON.—The term "foreign person" means—

(A) an individual who is not a United States person or an alien lawfully admitted for permanent residence into the United States; or

(B) a corporation, partnership, or other nongovernmental entity which is not a United States person.

(8) GOODS AND TECHNOLOGY.—The terms "goods" and "technology" have the meanings given those terms in section 16 of the Export Administration Act of 1979 (50 U.S.C. App. 2415).

(9) INVESTMENT.—The term "investment" means any of the following activities if such activity is undertaken pursuant to an agreement, or pursuant to the exercise of rights under such an agreement, that is entered into with the Government of Iran or a nongovenmental entity in Iran, or with the Government of Libya or a nongovernmental entity in Libya, on or after the date of the enactment of this Act:

(A) The entry into a contract that includes responsibility for the development of petroleum resources located in Iran or Libya (as the case may be), or the entry into a contract providing for the general supervision and guarantee of another person's performance of such a contract.

(B) The purchase of a share of ownership, including an equity interest, in that development.

(C) The entry into a contract providing for the participation in royalties, earnings, or profits in that development, without regard to the form of the participation.

The term "investment" does not include the entry into, performance, or financing of a contract to sell or purchase goods, services, or technology.

(10) IRAN.—The term "Iran" includes any agency or instrumentality of Iran.

(11) IRANIAN DIPLOMATS AND REPRESENTATIVES OF OTHER GOVERNMENT AND MILITARY OR QUASI-GOVERNMENTAL INSTITUTIONS OF IRAN.—The term "Iranian diplomats and representatives of other government and military or quasi-governmental institutions of Iran" includes employees, representatives, or affiliates of Iran's—

(A) Foreign Ministry;

(B) Ministry of Intelligence and Security;

(C) Revolutionary Guard Corps;

(D) Crusade for Reconstruction;

(E) Qods (Jerusalem) Forces;

(F) Interior Ministry;

(G) Foundation for the Oppressed and Disabled;

(H) Prophet's Foundation;

(I) June 5th Foundation;

(J) Martyr's Foundation;

(K) Islamic Propagation Organization; and

(L) Ministry of Islamic Guidance.

(13) NUCLEAR EXPLOSIVE DEVICE.—The term "nuclear explosive device" means any device, whether assembled or disassembled, that is designed to produce an instantaneous release of an amount of nuclear energy from special nuclear material (as defined in section 11(aa) of the Atomic Energy Act of 1954) that is greater than the amount of energy that would be released from the detonation of one pound of trinitrotoluene (TNT).

(14) PERSON.—The term "person" means—

(A) a natural person;

(B) a corporation, business association, partnership, society, trust, any other nongovernmental entity, organization, or group, and any governmental entity operating as a business enterprise; and

(C) any successor to any entity described in subparagraph (B).

(15) PETROLEUM RESOURCES.—The term "petroleum resources" includes petroleum and natural gas resources.

(16) UNITED STATES OR STATE.—The term "United States" or "State" means the several States, the District of Columbia, the Commonwealth of Puerto Rico, the Commonwealth of the Northern Mariana Islands, American Samoa, Guam, the United States Virgin Islands, and any other territory or possession of the United States.

(17) UNITED STATES PERSON.—The term "United States person" means—

> (A) a natural person who is a citizen of the United States or who owes permanent allegiance to the United States; and

> (B) a corporation or other legal entity which is organized under the laws of the United States, any State or territory thereof, or the District of Columbia, if natural persons described in subparagraph (A) own, directly or directly, more than 50 percent of the outstanding capital stock or other beneficial interest in such legal entity.

Approved August 5, 1996.

PRESIDENT BILL CLINTON, MESSAGE TO CONGRESS CONCERNING THE CONTINUATION OF THE NATIONAL EMERGENCY WITH RESPECT TO IRAN

March 17, 1997

I hereby report to the Congress on developments concerning the national emergency with respect to Iran that was declared in Executive Order 12957 of March 15, 1995, and matters relating to the measures in that order and in Executive Order 12959 of May 6, 1995. This report is submitted pursuant to section 204(c) of the International Emergency Economic Powers Act, 50 U.S.C. 1703(c) (IEEPA), section 401(c) of the National Emergencies Act, 50 U.S.C. 1641(c), and section 505(c) of the International Security and Development Cooperation Act of 1985, 22 U.S.C. 2349aa-9(c). This report discusses only matters concerning the national emergency with respect to Iran that was declared in Executive Order 12957 and does not deal with those relating to the emergency declared on November 14, 1979, in connection with the hostage crisis.

1. On March 15, 1995, I issued Executive Order 12957 (60 Fed. Reg. 14615, March 17, 1995) to declare a national emergency with respect to Iran pursuant to IEEPA, and to prohibit the financing, management, or supervision by United States persons of the development of Iranian petroleum resources.

This action was in response to actions and policies of the Government of Iran, including support for international terrorism, efforts to undermine the Middle East peace process, and the acquisition of weapons of mass destruction and the means to deliver them. A copy of the order was provided to the Speaker of the House and the President of the Senate by letter dated March 15, 1995.

Following the imposition of these restrictions with regard to the development of Iranian petroleum resources, Iran continued to engage in activities that represent a threat to the peace and security of all nations, including Iran's continuing support for international terrorism, its support for acts that undermine the Middle East peace process, and its intensified efforts to acquire weapons of mass destruction. On May 6, 1995, I issued Executive Order 12959 to further respond to the Iranian threat to the national security, foreign policy, and economy of the United States.

Executive Order 12959 (60 Fed. Reg. 24757, May 9, 1995) (1) prohibits exportation from the United States to Iran or to the Government of Iran of goods, technology, or services; (2) prohibits the reexportation of certain U.S. goods and technology to Iran from third countries; (3) prohibits dealings by United States persons in goods and services of Iranian origin or owned or controlled by the Government of Iran; (4) prohibits new investments by United States persons in Iran or in property owned or controlled by the Government of Iran; (5) prohibits U.S. companies and other United States persons from approving, facilitating, or financing performance by a foreign subsidiary or other entity owned or controlled by a United States person of certain reexport, investment, and trade transactions that a United States person is prohibited from performing; (6) continues the 1987 prohibition on the importation into the United States of goods and services of Iranian origin; (7) prohibits any transaction by a United States person or within the United States that evades or avoids or attempts to violate any prohibition of the order; and (8) allowed U.S. companies a 30-day period in which to perform trade transactions pursuant to contracts predating the Executive order.

At the time of signing Executive Order 12959, I directed the Secretary of the Treasury to authorize through specific licensing certain transactions, including transactions by United States persons related to the Iran-United States Claims Tribunal in The Hague, established pursuant to the Algiers Accords, and related to other international obligations and United States Government functions, and transactions related to the export of agricultural commodities pursuant to preexisting contracts consistent with section 5712(c) of title 7, United States Code. I also directed the Secretary of the Treasury, in consultation with the Secretary of State, to consider authorizing United States persons through specific licensing to participate in market-based swaps of crude oil from the Caspian Sea area for Iranian crude oil in support of energy projects in Azerbaijan, Kazakstan, and Turkmenistan.

Executive Order 12959 revoked sections 1 and 2 of Executive Order 12613 of October 29, 1987, and sections 1 and 2 of Executive Order 12957 of March 15, 1995, to the extent they are inconsistent with it. A copy of Executive Order 12959 was transmitted to the Speaker of the House of Representatives and the President of the Senate by letter dated May 6, 1995.

2. On March 5, 1997, I renewed for another year the national emergency with respect to Iran pursuant to IEEPA. This renewal extended the authority for the current comprehensive trade embargo against Iran in effect since May 1995. Under these sanctions, virtually all trade with Iran is prohibited except for information and informational materials and certain other limited exceptions.

3. The Iranian Transactions Regulations (the "Regulations" or ITR), 31 CFR Part 560, were amended on October 21, 1996 (61 Fed. Reg. 54936, October 23, 1996), to implement section 4 of the Federal Civil Penalties Inflation Adjustment Act of 1990, as amended by the Debt Collection Improvement Act of 1996, by adjusting for inflation the amount of the civil monetary penalties that may be assessed under the Regulations. The amendment increases the maximum civil monetary penalty provided in the Regulations from $10,000 to $11,000 per violation.

The amended Regulations also reflect an amendment to 18 U.S.C. 1001 contained in section 330016(1)(L) of Public Law 103-322, September 13, 1994; 108 Stat. 2147. The amendment notes the availability of higher criminal fines pursuant to the formulas set forth in 18 U.S.C. 3571. A copy of the amendment is attached.

Section 560.603 of the ITR was amended on November 15, 1996 (61 Fed. Reg. 58480), to clarify rules relating to reporting requirements imposed on United States persons with foreign affiliations. Initial reporting under the amended Regulation has been deferred until May 30, 1997, by a January 14, 1997 Federal Register notice (62 Fed. Reg. 1832). Copies of the amendment and the notice are attached.

4. During the current 6-month period, the Department of the Treasury's Office of Foreign Assets Control (OFAC) made numerous decisions with respect to applications for licenses to engage in transactions under the ITR, and issued 13 licenses. The majority of denials were in response to requests to authorize commercial exports to Iran—particularly of machinery and equipment for the petroleum and manufacturing industries—and the importation of Iranian-origin goods. The licenses issued authorized the export and reexport of goods, services, and technology essential to ensure the safety of civil aviation and safe operation of certain commercial passenger aircraft in Iran; certain financial and legal transactions; the importation of Iranian-origin artwork for public exhibition; and certain diplomatic transactions. Pursuant to sections 3 and 4 of Executive Order 12959 and in order to comply with the Iran-Iraq Arms Non-Proliferation Act of 1992 and other statutory restrictions applicable to certain goods and technology, including those involved in the air-safety cases, the Department of the Treasury continues to consult with the Departments of State and Commerce on these matters.

The U.S. financial community continues to interdict transactions associated with Iran and to consult with OFAC about their appropriate handling. Many of these inquiries have resulted in investigations into the activities of U.S. parties and, where appropriate, the initiation of enforcement action.

5. The U.S. Customs Service has continued to effect numerous seizures of Iranian-origin merchandise, primarily carpets, for violation of the import prohibitions of the ITR. Various enforcement actions carried over from previous reporting periods are continuing, and new reports of violations are being aggressively pursued. Since my last report, OFAC has collected a civil monetary penalty in the amount of $5,000. The violation underlying this collection involves the unlicensed import of Iranian-origin goods for transshipment to a third country aboard a U.S.-flag vessel. Civil penalty action or review is pending against 21 companies, financial institutions, and individuals for possible violations of the Regulations.

6. The expenses incurred by the Federal Government in the 6-month period from September 15, 1996, through March 14, 1997, that are directly attributable to the exercise of powers and authorities conferred by the declaration of a national emergency with respect to Iran are approximately $800,000, most of which represent wage and salary costs for Federal personnel. Personnel costs were largely centered in the Department of the Treasury (particularly in the Office of Foreign Assets Control, The U.S. Customs Service, the Office of the Under Secretary for Enforcement, and the Office of the General Counsel), the Department of State (particularly the Bureau of Economic and Business Affairs, the Bureau of Near Eastern Affairs, the Bureau of Intelligence and Research, and the Office of the Legal Adviser), and the Department of Commerce (the Bureau of Export Administration and the General Counsel's Office).

7. The situation reviewed above continues to involve important diplomatic, financial, and legal interests of the United States and its nationals and presents an extraordinary and unusual threat to the national security, foreign policy, and economy of the United States. The declaration of the national emergency with respect to Iran contained in Executive Order 12957 and the comprehensive economic sanctions imposed by Executive Order 12959 underscore the United States Government opposition to the actions and policies of the Government of Iran, particularly its support of international terrorism and its efforts to acquire weapons of mass destruction and the means to deliver them. The Iranian Transactions Regulations issued pursuant to Executive Orders 12957 and 12959 continue to advance important objectives in promoting the nonproliferation and antiterrorism policies of the United States. I shall exercise the powers at my disposal to deal with these problems and will report periodically to the Congress on significant developments.

ZE'EV SCHIFF, "BIG STICK AND A SMALL CARROT: ARE CHANGES IN ISRAELI AND U.S. POLICIES TOWARD IRAN IN THE MAKING?"

Ha'aretz, December 13, 1996

Is a process presently taking place to bring about change in Israeli and U.S. policies toward Israel's most threatening enemy Iran? Were such a change to take place, it would be viewed as revolutionary and yet, there are some signs in Israel and the United States that this may be occurring. In the last few months, no vehement calls have been heard in Israel against Iran and its regime.

What is happening backstage? Since less threatening pronouncements have been made in Israel against Iran, foreign countries have recently turned to Israel to find out whether a change had indeed taken place. It turns out, that Israel sent mixed messages on the Iranian issue. Jerusalem conveyed to some of its embassies the message that they should not respond to requests regarding a possible policy change by Israel toward Iran. The order is to neither confirm nor deny. It follows that Israel is interested in leaving the issue in a fog. Even if nothing is happening, Israel is pleased by the accounts that change may be taking place—only apparently.

On another track, Israel recently conveyed different messages to a few Arab countries in the Persian Gulf. The Gulf countries certainly thought that the simultaneity of the Israeli and U.S. statements on possible policy change toward Iran were no coincidence. The Iraqis, for instance, explain that the change was initiated by Israel in order to incorporate Iran in its onslaught against the Arabs. The message that was conveyed to those countries was that there was no change. There may be some change in rhetoric, but Israel's policy toward the Iranian threat remains as it was.

Saudi Arabia had asked a similar question. As accounts proliferate that Israel has maintained links with Iraq, the Saudis have voiced their concerns to Washington. President Clinton raised these concerns in turn with the late Prime Minister Yitzhak Rabin. In Martin Indyk's first speech after his appointment as U.S. Ambassador to Israel, he referred to a possible Israeli-Iraqi rapprochement and forcefully suggested that Israel be careful.

There is a substantial difference between Israel and the United States concerning a radical change in the policy toward Iran: it is doubtful whether Israel can modify its policy while the United States carries on with its previous policy. Israel cannot afford what France and Germany allowed themselves in their relationships with Iran. Future Iranian intimidations, too, are understood differently in Israel and in the United States There was no change in the Israeli assessment of those threats that would have justified a modification of basic policy. This policy heavily dictates Israel's stance on its readiness to sign the nuclear non-proliferation treaty.

Notwithstanding this, it would have been better for Israel to reexamine the nature of the occasional threatening proclamations by Israeli personalities; too bad this was not done during Rabin's time, when senior IDF officers uttered a series of threats in succession as well. The acquisition of F15-Es, was also explained by the need to hit remote targets in Iran. This is how Israel placed itself needlessly at the forefront of the planners of military actions against Iran. Tehran perceives Israel as inciting Washington to acts of force against Iran and as standing behind international moves against it.

Israel is greatly in need of the United States to fight possible Iranian threats. A change in the United States' Iran policy would cause a shock in Israel if it is not coordinated with Jerusalem. Even if Iranian slogans dub Israel "the small Satan" and the United States "the great Satan," it is clear that Iran's struggle with the United States is based mostly on strategic interests. As concerns Israel, however, Iranian strategic appraisals are combined with religious and ideological reasons. The difference is substantial. Even if Israel signaled its desire for a change in relations, it is doubtful whether Iran would be ready for it. If Israel signs a peace treaty with Syria and the Palestinians, there might be some softening of the relations with Iran, but nothing more than that will occur.

Washington had always been ready for an open dialogue with Iran, not a covert operation like the Iran-Contra affair—it was Iran which rejected the overt track.

Checks with the various branches of the U.S. administration reveal that no comprehensive discussion of the U.S. Iran policy has been conducted for months. Such a debate will certainly take place, but the claim that new Iran-related decisions have already been made is baseless This said, it is obvious that, under the surface, embers are glowing in Washington. There are question-marks about the Iran policy and also a malaise in various circles such as the U.S. business community. The question-marks proliferated after the United States failure in northern Iraq, when Saddam Hussein was assisting the Kurdish faction (PDK) headed by Massud Barazani.

A major problem is whether the "dual containment" policy toward Iran and Iraq has failed in practice. Most experts affirm that the pressure on Saddam Hussein should not be lifted, but this is not the case with Iran. Some experts say that the containment policy toward Iran hurt its economy, slowed down its arms procurements, but also pushed Iran into extremism and upset the relations between Washington and some of its European friends. They—and others —say it is high time for a reexamination of the dual containment policy

Since 1995, Washington has intensified its policy toward Iran, first of all by escalating the sanctions: they reached their peak in August 1996, when a presidential order called for the boycott of foreign companies dealing with the Iranian—and Libyan—energy industries if they invested more than 40 million dollars. European countries that had until then supported the United States' Iranian policy (such as the United Kingdom, Norway and Denmark) distanced themselves from the measure. Questions did recently arise in Germany whether that country's "constructive dialogue" with Iran has been successful, but Germany's Iranian policy has not changed. U. S. businessmen remark that the Europeans are making deals while the United States pays the price for its policy. This is why the policy must be revised.

An example of the contradiction in the U.S. policy toward Iran can be found in the issue of the oil and gas pipelines from Azerbaijan, Kazakhstan, and Turkmenistan that large oil conglomerates plan to build. Those countries have huge oil reserves, the importance of which will grow; to make their export possible, large pipelines must be laid. The U.S. interest is to lay as many pipelines as possible to reduce dependence and risks. The United States ruled out Iran's participation because of its sanctions policy and is pressuring the other countries to do the same. There are a few alternatives to laying the pipelines, for instance through Georgia, Turkey, and Russia, the irony of the matter being, according to some experts, that Washington this way stimulates the collaboration of various countries with Russia. This would strengthen Russia, giving it strategic control of the oil routes. All this in order to deny Iran any profits.

The U.S. policy vis-à-vis Iran cannot be analyzed in terms of any single factor. A change in U.S.-Iranian policy is linked to other issues such as Saudi Arabia's position, for example. The problem is not just whether this will influence Saddam Hussein's Iraq, but Kuwait and other friends of the United States too. One of those, the United Arab Emirates, has a territorial dispute with Iran over three islands. A positive U.S. signal to Iran would weaken the U.A.E.'s stance. The U.S. policy vis-à-vis Iran is also linked with its relations with Turkey, presently headed by a Prime Minister from the Islamic Party. It follows that if a reassessment is to be expected in Washington, it will be a appraisal encompassing the whole Mideast, the Persian Gulf, and the Muslim Republics, in which Iran will only constitute one of the issues.

Some ex-CIA experts make the same comments. They say that a big power like the United States cannot be left to operate with only one option (against Iran) without allowing the other side the opportunity to choose another policy as well. They contend that Washington must also offer Iran positive incentives if it agrees to change its policy: for instance, clarify to Tehran that the United States could withdraw its opposition to Iran's integration in the pipeline project (by letting the lines cross Iran), if it can prove that it does not support terrorism and is not working to obtain weapons of mass destruction. This way it would be possible, with the cooperation of European countries, to submit Iran to tests that, were they not passed, would legitimate a broader sanction policy. One of the experts opined that such a change could be obtained from the Iranians, but if it turned out that in spite of everything, Iran went on developing nuclear weapons, there would be no choice but to use U.S. military force against the installations.

Therefore, the new assessment is in an early stage. It is slowly forming at various levels in Washington, within and outside the administration. Israel is but a tiny element in this big scheme, but one should not conclude that it cannot influence those within the Beltway. Israel's voice must be heard precisely because Iranian terrorism struck it more than others and because nuclear weapons in Iran's hands might endanger its existence.

INTERVIEW WITH GERMAN FOREIGN MINISTER KLAUS KINKEL IN THE WAKE OF THE BERLIN COURT VERDICT IN THE MYKONOS TRIAL

Michael J. Inacker, Hamburg Welt am Sonntag, April 13, 1997

Inacker: How do you assess the verdict by the Berlin court in the Mykonos trial concerning Germany's policy toward Iran?

Kinkel: The verdict by the Berlin court includes statements that will certainly have an impact on Germany's policy toward Iran. The involvement of official Iranian authorities in the armed attack on the Mykonos restaurant in Berlin, mentioned in the verdict, is a blatant violation of international law.

Inacker: What does the suspension of the critical dialogue mean? Can we expect more far-reaching steps against Iran?

Kinkel: The verdict must have consequences for Germany's foreign policy. For this reason, we have recalled our ambassador and suspended the critical dialogue. Our European partners, with the exception of Greece, have displayed solidarity. On 29 April, we want to discuss our future policy vis-á-vis Iran. A reevaluation is now necessary. Everything else will now depend on the behavior of the Iranian leadership. It must strictly obey the rules of international law. In any event, we do not want to break off relations with Iran, which have lasted for over 100 years, and, in spite of our dismay, we do no want to add fuel to the fire.

Inacker: What are the consequences for the security of German citizens in Iran and for security in Germany?

Kinkel: We are taking Foreign Minister Velayati at his word: Last week he said that there is no need to be concerned about the secu-

---

Reprinted with permission from the Hamburg *Welt am Sonntag*, April 13, 1997, p. 3.

rity of the Germans and other European foreigners living in Germany. The same applies to Iranian citizens living in Germany. By the way, we ourselves have naturally also taken all the necessary precautionary measures. People in Germany need not be afraid of terrorist attacks.

Inacker: What about the consequences for economic relations between Germany and Iran?

Kinkel: As far as economic relations are concerned, they will have to orient themselves toward the results of the reevaluation of our future policy toward Iran. In this area, too, a calm assessment is needed.

Inacker: What impact will the verdict have on the relationship between the West and the Islamic states against the background of the debate on the "war of the cultures?"

Kinkel: A "war of the cultures" would be the most stupid thing that could happen. I have always advocated a dialogue with the representatives of the Islamic states that are ready for dialogue. All the cultures on this earth—the Western civilization, Islam, or Hinduism, to mention only three—have only one planet on which they are living together. Thus, I do not think much of the thesis of an unavoidable "war of the cultures." We should know much more about each other and try to promote mutual understanding. In any event, I for my part am ready to do so.

Inacker: Will the verdict lead to a new yardstick for the relationship between human rights and foreign policy?

Kinkel: Human rights are and will continue to be a central pillar of German foreign policy. This principle corresponds to our constitution and our view of the world. There is no need to relativize this goal. Yet it is quite necessary to think about how the objectives of a committed human rights policy can best be pursued. As far as the relationship with Iran is concerned, the EU heads of state and government decided in December 1992 that a dialogue with the Iranian Government should be continued, in spite of the well-known allegations. Within this framework, concern about Iran's behavior was to be expressed, and efforts were to be made to achieve improvements. The underlying idea was: It is better to talk to each other than face each other silently. The critical dialogue is not and never was the hobby of the Federal Government. It was and is a European decision.

Inacker: Has our foreign policy really benefited from the dialogue?

Kinkel: A few things have been achieved. I would like to mention the following examples: The adoption of the chemical weapons convention by Iran, Iran's approval of the extension of the Nonproliferation Treaty, cooperation between the Iranian Government and the International Atomic Energy Agency, the release of German and other West European hostages in Lebanon, the pardon and later release of a German sentenced to death in Iran, the verbal promise that Iran will not send any killer commands against writer Salman Rushdie, and the resumption of cooperation between Iran and the special U.N. rapporteurs for human rights issues.

Inacker: Should such a dialogue not be halted if a state directs its aggression toward the territory of other states?

Kinkel: There can be no dialogue "at any price." There are limits that are reached when international law and the sovereignty of another country are massively violated. For this reason, a reaction was necessary. This has happened. Iran must respect international law and abide by it. Both sides must then think about a new beginning.

STATEMENT OF THE FOREIGN MINISTERS OF THE GULF COOPERATION COUNCIL (EXCERPTS)

March 26, 1997

Their excellencies the foreign ministers of the Gulf Cooperation Council [GCC] member states ended the 62nd session of the GCC ministerial council today. The meeting started yesterday evening at the general secretariat of the council in Riyad, under the chairmanship of the foreign minister of Qatar, Shaykh Hamad Bin Jasim [Bin] Jabr Al Thani.

H.R.H. Minister of Foreign Affairs Prince Sa'ud al-Faysal chaired the delegation of the Kingdom of Saudi Arabia to this session.

At the end of the meetings, the GCC ministerial council issued the following statement:

The ministerial council reviewed the developments of the joint course and issues [of the GCC] cooperation and the current political and security issues at the regional and international levels since the convening of the 17th session of the GCC higher council in Doha last December.

On Iraq's implementation of the U.N. Security Council's resolutions on its aggression against the State of Kuwait:

The ministerial council has reviewed the developments in Iraq's implementation of the U.N. Security Council's resolutions on its aggression against Kuwait. It expresses satisfaction with the implementation of Resolution 986 on oil-for-food as it means a reduction in the sufferings of the Iraqi people, which has been continuously called for by the ministerial council. It calls on Iraq to be committed to and

---

to seriously and sincerely cooperate in guaranteeing the precise and sound implementation of that resolution, with the hope that the difficulties facing the supply of foodstuffs and medicines in the shortest time possible will be overcome. That will contribute to the improvement of the regrettable living and health conditions of the Iraqi people for which the Iraqi government is solely responsible.

The ministerial council has noticed with every regret the fact that the Iraqi government has continued to follow its policies of procrastination and evasion with regard to the need to implement essential and general aspects of the U.N. Security Council's resolutions. At the forefront of these resolutions is the need to free more than 600 prisoners and hostages from the State of Kuwait and other states, to abide by the compensation mechanism, to return public and private Kuwaiti property and refrain from any hostile or provocative moves or acts against the State of Kuwait and the other neighbouring states, in implementation of Resolution 949.

The ministerial council has expressed its anxiety with regard to the Iraqi government's continuing to hide a number of missiles and chemical and biological weapons banned under Resolutions 687 and 707, and its hampering of the work of the U.N. Special Commission.

The ministerial council has reiterated the GCC member states' readiness to continue to contribute so as to give financial, political and moral support to the commission. In this context, it calls on the international community to continue to back the efforts of that commission so as to make its work successful and ensure the implementation of the U.N. resolutions aimed at eliminating all the Iraqi mass destruction weapons.

The ministerial council reiterated its sympathy with the Iraqi people and its firm stance regarding the need to preserve Iraq's independence and sovereignty, and the unity of its territory and its regional security.

The issue of the occupation of the U.A.E.'s three islands:

The ministerial council reviewed the recent developments on the issue of Iran's occupation of the U.A.E.'s three islands—Greater and Lesser Tunb and Abu Musa.

[135]

Noting the Iranian government's continuation in carrying out measures aimed at consolidating its occupation of the three islands and going to the extremes of pursuing the imposition of the fait accompli by force, which constituted a determination to continue in its unjustifiable provocative steps, the council reiterated its serious regret over the continuation of the Islamic Republic of Iran in abstaining from responding to the repeated, sincere and serious invitations issued by the U.A.E. and other regional and international organizations, bodies and gatherings which called for resolving this conflict peacefully.

The ministerial council also expressed its denunciation of the consecutive Iranian measures over the U.A.E.'s islands and its concern at the consequences of the Iranian government's determination to pursue the imposition of a fait accompli policy by force in the three islands of Greater and Lesser Tunb and Abu Musa, which constitutes a violation of the U.A.E.'s sovereignty and an infringement on its rights to these islands, endangers security and stability in the region, and contradicts the principles and conventions of international law, the U.N. Charter, the Organization of the Islamic Conference, and the principles of good neighbourliness and respect for the sovereignty and unity of countries of the regions.

While the ministerial council renews its emphasis on the U.A.E.'s sovereignty over its three islands—Greater and Lesser Tunb and Abu Musa, and its absolute backing for all the measures it takes and peaceful means it uses for the reimposition of its sovereignty over these islands, the council repeated its call to the Iranian government to terminate its occupation of the three islands, refrain from exercising the imposition of the fait accompli policy by force, cease to build Iranian installations on the islands with the aim of changing their demographic structure, abolish all measures [last three words as heard], remove all the installations implemented unilaterally earlier in the three islands and pursue peaceful means for solving the conflict over them in accordance with the principles and conventions of international law, including accepting the referral of the issue to the International Court of Justice.

Relations with Iran:

The ministerial council reviewed the development of relations with the Islamic Republic of Iran, proceeding from its constant position based on its keen wish to found these relations on good neighbourliness, commitment to the principles of mutual respect, non-interference in the domestic affairs of others, shunning the use of force or the threat to use force, and resolving differences by peaceful means in accordance with the principles and rules of international law, and the need to meet the requirements of maintaining security and stability of the region.

While welcoming the new trends expressed by the foreign minister of the Islamic Republic of Iran during his recent tour in the council member states, and the affirmations of the Iranian leadership in its recent contacts with the council member states, the council expresses the preparedness of member states to respond positively to these trends and affirmations, and to take serious action for building trust and putting relations between the two sides on the correct course politically and in the field of information.

EMIRATES CENTER FOR STRATEGIC STUDIES AND RESEARCH, "GULF SECURITY FROM A NATIONAL PERSPECTIVE"

Summary of Conference Proceedings, Abu Dhabi, United Arab Emirates, April 5–6, 1997

The Emirates Center for Strategic Studies and Research (ECSSR) in Abu Dhabi, the United Arab Emirates, provided the Council on Foreign Relations with a summary of the proceedings of a conference the ECSSR hosted on "Gulf Security from a National Perspective" on April 5–6, 1997. This conference, in which 80 high-level officials, academics, and journalists from the Gulf Cooperation Council (GCC) countries participated, was a unique and comprehensive attempt to look, from an internal perspective, at the wide range of views on the many topics that relate to Gulf security. The agenda itself was divided into six panels, each featuring a main presentation and followed by an open discussion period. A final roundtable discussion served as the concluding session.

THE FIRST PANEL:

> "AN ANALYTICAL STUDY OF GULF
> SECURITY FROM THE PERSPECTIVE OF
> *DESERT WARRIOR* BY H.R.H. PRINCE
> KHALID BIN SULTAN BIN ABDELAZIZ
> AL-SAUD"
> DR. MUHAMMAD JABBER AL-ANSARI,
> BAHRAIN

The first panel opened with a presentation on the book *Desert Warrior* authored by H.R.H. Prince Khalid Bin Sultan Bin Abdelaziz Al-Saud, in which the question of Gulf security was addressed. As the presentation made clear, the events of 1990 need to be careful-

[138]

ly studied in order to preclude the emergence of any similar external threats arising again. Among the prerequisites born out of such a view is the need for further cooperation among the GCC member states, better use of the available internal resources, and the undertaking of necessary domestic reforms in each respective country. The new world environment demands that all Gulf countries are well prepared in order to be able to meet its challenges. Regional cooperation and security can only be discussed as a whole and by all affected countries, including Iran and Iraq once they adopt a changed attitude. Panel One argued that while "dual containment" should be replaced by "dual rehabilitation," strategic flexibility and combat readiness remain essential requisites to the security of the region.

THE SECOND PANEL:

> "GCC DEFENSE POLICIES: FACTS,
> CHALLENGES, POSSIBILITIES"
> BRIGADIER HAYEL JUMAH AL-HAMLY,
> UNITED ARAB EMIRATES

Panel Two examined a number of facts, challenges, and possibilities in terms of present GCC defense policies. It highlighted the strategic importance of the Gulf region in historical, political, economic, and cultural terms before moving onto the regional threats facing the GCC countries. Reference was made to common Arab defense initiatives such as the Joint Arab Defense Pact, the Damascus Declaration, the proposed "Peninsula Shield" force, and the common Gulf army. Recommendations made for common GCC security in this panel included closing ranks and ending differences, addressing GCC border disputes, developing the Damascus Declaration formula especially in the military domain, increasing diplomatic ties between the GCC and Iran, establishing a unified GCC position in Arab, Islamic, and international circles, and adopting an integrated approach to security and military agreements between GCC states on the one hand and their friends and allies on the other. Focusing on military issues, the presentation stressed the need for a common defense strategy, joint military research, education and training, better communication systems, and improved GCC military capabilities. The "Peninsula Shield" force is of particular importance in this regard.

THE THIRD PANEL:

> "INTERNAL SECURITY CHALLENGES
> FACING GCC COUNTRIES"
> DR. MUHAMMAD AL-RUMAIHI, KUWAIT

The topic of Panel Three was the security challenges facing the GCC countries assessed from an independent, national perspective. The presentation dealt with both internal and external challenges and with the recognition that the regional and national interests of the GCC countries are inseparable. It also focused on the relationship between the GCC states and the major world powers, particularly the United States and Britain, and their vested interest in guaranteeing a sustained flow of oil to the international markets. The third panel pointed to the fact that the Gulf region remains one of the most tense areas in the world. Its great value as a rich oil resource and a thriving consumer market, the opportunities it offers to expatriates in terms of job openings, and its unique land and naval location all make it susceptible to regional and great power disputes. The current fragile state of Middle East politics in general adds additional challenges toward the promotion of peace and stability of the Gulf, particularly in the form of the rise of Shi'ite political Islam and Arab nationalism. There are also internal security threats posed by economic, ideological, and political factors. It is therefore important to develop a sense of common awareness that transcends narrow and individual interests into broader and more sustainable ones.

"REGIONAL THREATS AND
INTERNATIONAL INTERFERENCE IN THE
GULF REGION"
DR. JAMAL SANAD AL-SUWAIDI, UNITED
ARAB EMIRATES

Panel Four examined regional threats and international interference, suggesting that there is a steady relationship between Gulf security and the stability of the international scene. Establishing peace in and around the Gulf region may be conducive to a more stable international order. However, the situation of Gulf security in 1997 remains uncertain for the following reasons:

- the continued Iranian occupation of the Abu Musa and the Greater and Lesser Tunbs islands of the United Arab Emirates;

- Iran's ongoing military acquisition program and its continued efforts to acquire weapons of mass destruction;

- Iran's opposition to the Arab-Israeli peace process.

A careful and objective study of the issue of Gulf security requires the following to be taken into consideration:

- the collapse of the Arab regional order, and the failure of the Arab League and other regional organizations to accept the second Gulf War crisis in 1990;

- the "dual containment" policy and its implications, the continued international sanctions imposed on Iraq, the existing conflict between the United States and Iran, and the possibility of its development into an open confrontation;

- the disintegration of the former Soviet Union and the new conditions of the post–Cold War era;

- the deterioration of the Iranian economy.

While deeper and firmer cooperation among the GCC countries is required to respond to the above considerations, measures of confidence-building as far as Iran is concerned need also to be incorporated. GCC members should rely more on their own resources in terms of planning the security of the region.

THE FIFTH PANEL:

> "GCC RELATIONS WITH ARAB
> COUNTRIES"
> DR. SALEH AL-MANI, KINGDOM OF
> SAUDI ARABIA

The fifth panel considered the relationship between the GCC and other Arab countries both in their official and non-official forms, and identified the following general dimensions:

- a political dimension represented by the alliances and diplomatic relations that are of particular importance to Arab countries engaged in direct negotiations with Israel;

- a politico-economic dimension represented by the flow of trade, aid, and investments;

- an ideological dimension represented by the common culture which transcends political barriers.

At present, there are three factors that influence the nature of relations between the GCC and other Arab countries:

- the idea that strong economic GCC-Arab relations will eventually lead to stronger political ties;

- the myth of the inevitable Arab unity created by the historical urge to reconstruct the glories of the past, either in its religious form of a "Caliphate" or in its political form of a unitary centralized state;

- the conviction held by certain GCC intellectuals that the Gulf can do without the rest of the Arab world, ignoring the existence of the strong cultural ties that bind them together.

The presentation noted that inter-GCC and GCC-Arab relations have become pragmatic only since the mid-20th century. These relations cannot be separated from equations of power and interest. The GCC and other Arab countries are still highly influenced by memories of the cold wars of the sixties and the outrageous wars of the nineties. Although the former have largely subsided, the possibility that they may reemerge cannot be totally excluded. A practical political framework is therefore essential to prevent such a conflagration. New mechanisms are also needed to build a new and firm Arab security framework that does not only address the relations between the Arab world and Israel but also the bilateral relations among the Arab countries themselves.

THE SIXTH PANEL:

"ECONOMIC CHALLENGES FACING GCC COUNTRIES"
DR. ABDULLAH EL-KUWAIZ, KINGDOM OF SAUDI ARABIA

The economic challenges and opportunities facing the GCC were dealt with during the sixth panel. Highlighting the exceptional economic performance of the GCC countries, this presentation noted that the GCC member states have built modern social and economic structures in a relatively short time and in spite of adverse economic circumstances and political instability. As far as the main challenges facing the GCC countries are concerned, the following areas were identified:

• population growth and social problems;

• the need for better financial and monetary systems and for reformed economic management;

• the challenges posed by economic globalization and regional organizations.

The GCC countries have sound health and education policies and their living standards and per capita income rates are high. But the rapid population growth remains a problem that requires clear-cut policies to meet economic and social needs. The high percentage of expatriates working in the area is another demographic problem that cannot be ignored.

As a result of globalization, a number of other studies have forecast a higher economic growth rate for the GCC. Demand on oil, for example, is predicted to rise and restrictions on other main exports of the GCC, such as petrochemicals, are expected to be eased. However, the presentation cautioned that the GCC countries remain susceptible to the negative implications of globalization because of their dependence on oil as their main international export. A well-structured plan to diversify the GCC economies is therefore a high priority. In turn, the presentation made the following set of recommendations:

- pursuing efforts to improve educational systems;

- raising the costs of expatriate recruitment to encourage employers to focus more on the skills and potential of the GCC nationals;

- setting the GCC house in order, financially speaking, to meet the large rises in education and health-care costs;

- privatizing industries and services as a means of raising more funds for the treasury and reducing the annual government expenditures;

- applying a sales tax and raising customs duties;

- improving investment conditions for the benefit of both national and international investors. Current GCC investment laws should be reconsidered to remove existing legal obstacles.

Background Materials

"ROUNDTABLE DISCUSSION ON GULF
SECURITY"
H.R.H. PRINCE KHALID BIN SULTAN BIN
ABDELAZIZ AL-SAUD, KINGDOM OF
SAUDI ARABIA

The conference concluded with its seventh panel and a roundtable discussion of the overall conference theme. Recognizing a multiplicity of definitions of the concept of security itself, the panel speaker defined Gulf security as "providing peace and stability by avoiding any internal or external disruption of the status quo." GCC security, meanwhile, was defined as "the strategic end of the GCC countries to meet national interests determined by the GCC political leaderships, protect the existence, survival, sovereignty, and international standing of the countries of the region and ensure their active involvement in building Arab national security in general."

A number of threats facing the region were then identified, including border disputes, Iranian expansionism, Iraq's hibernating ambitions, the persistence of a destabilizing armament race, the possible dangers of terrorism, extremism and violence, the self-serving Israeli practices, and the unconditional U.S. support of Israel. The discussion moved quickly to the main players in the region and their respective versions of Gulf security. Iran favors independence and territorial sovereignty and rejects foreign interference in the security arrangements of the region. Iraq remains a potential threat as long as Saddam remains in power, but it will not be in a position to deliver any effective strike unless sanctions are lifted and control over its air space is fully restored. Turkey's version of Gulf and Middle East security is based on its conviction that this should be the sole concern of the countries of the region. Meanwhile, the United States has large interests in the region that will be served by the continuation of the current state of "uncontrolled instability." In recent years, Israel has begun to figure as a new, seriously intrusive player in the arena of Gulf security. Finally, Russia and France, each with an agenda aimed at boosting economic ties and maintaining political and strategic leverage in the region, need also to be considered.

The panel concluded with a set of practical recommendations:

- *On the GCC level:* a security plan is needed that includes all economic, military, social and political elements. Deterrence weapons should be acquired, decision making tools improved and democratic practices enhanced. A common military leadership could be established to steer operations of GCC forces in the field of deterrence and reaction to actual threats.

- *On the Arab world level:* Gulf security must be tied to the Red Sea and Arab national security in general. Inter-Arab differences must also be resolved.

- *On the regional level:* the GCC member states should adopt a more open approach to Iran based on mutual interests and a specific stance toward Iraq taking into account possible future scenarios. In addition, regional organizations should be created and empowered to settle disputes by peaceful means.

- *On the international level:* the European, Russian and Chinese roles must be recognized, while efforts need to be made to direct the region away from international conflicts.

The GCC countries must make a clear decision as to whether they wish to give priority to their respective national security, the local security of the GCC countries alone, or the wider concept of Gulf security that involves all the countries surrounding the Gulf.